The Boys

McFarland Classics

1997–1998

Archer. *Willis O'Brien* • Cline. *In the Nick of Time* • Frasier. *Russ Meyer—The Life and Films* • Hayes. *3-D Movies* • Hayes. *Trick Cinematography* • Hogan. *Dark Romance* • Holland. *B Western Actors Encyclopedia* • Jarlett. *Robert Ryan* • McGee. *Roger Corman* • Okuda & Watz. *The Columbia Comedy Shorts* • Pitts. *Western Movies* • Selby. *Dark City* • Warren. *Keep Watching the Skies!* • West. *Television Westerns*

1999–2000

Benson. *Vintage Science Fiction Films, 1896–1949* • Cline. *Serials-ly Speaking* • Darby & Du Bois. *American Film Music* • Hayes. *The Republic Chapterplays* • Hill. *Raymond Burr* • Horner. *Bad at the Bijou* • Kinnard. *Horror in Silent Films* • McGhee. *John Wayne* • Nowlan. *Cinema Sequels and Remakes, 1903–1987* • Okuda. *The Monogram Checklist* • Parish. *Prison Pictures from Hollywood* • Sigoloff. *The Films of the Seventies* • Slide. *Nitrate Won't Wait* • Tropp. *Images of Fear* • Tuska. *The Vanishing Legion* • Watson. *Television Horror Movie Hosts* • Weaver. *Poverty Row HORRORS!* • Weaver. *Return of the B Science Fiction and Horror Heroes*

2001

Byrge & Miller. *The Screwball Comedy Films* • Chesher. *"The End"* • Erickson. *Religious Radio and Television in the United States, 1921–1991* • Fury. *Kings of the Jungle* • Galbraith. *Motor City Marquees* • Langman & Gold. *Comedy Quotes from the Movies* • Levine. *The 247 Best Movie Scenes in Film History* • McGee. *Beyond Ballyhoo* • Mank. *Hollywood Cauldron* • Martin. *The Allied Artists Checklist* • Nollen. *The Boys* • Quarles. *Down and Dirty* • Smith. *Famous Hollywood Locations* • Watz. *Wheeler & Woolsey*

THE BOYS

The Cinematic World
of Laurel and Hardy

by
Scott Allen Nollen

with a foreword by
JOHN McCABE

McFarland Classics

McFarland & Company, Inc., Publishers
Jefferson, North Carolina, and London

The present work is a reprint of the library bound edition of
The Boys: The Cinematic World of Laurel and Hardy, *first
published in 1989. McFarland Classics is an imprint of
McFarland & Company, Inc., Publishers, Jefferson, North
Carolina, who also published the original edition.*

*Frontispiece: Ollie and Stan in the 1939 Boris Morros production
for RKO-Radio,* The Flying Deuces.

Library of Congress Cataloguing-in-Publication Data

Nollen, Scott Allen.
   The boys.

   Filmography: p. 93.
   Bibliography: p. 149.
    Includes index.
    ISBN 0-7864-1115-5 (softcover : 50# alkaline paper) ∞
    1. Laurel, Stan.   2. Hardy, Oliver, 1892–1957.
   3. Comedians—United States—Biography.   4. Motion
picture actors and actresses—United States—Biography.
   I. Title.
   PN2287.L285N65   2001   791.43'028'0922 [B]   89-42742

British Library cataloguing data are available

Manufactured in the United States of America

*McFarland & Company, Inc., Publishers
  Box 611, Jefferson, North Carolina 28640
  www.mcfarlandpub.com*

This book is dedicated to all people
who have laughed at a Laurel and Hardy film.
It is also dedicated to those who have not done so,
in the hope that, after reading this, they will

Foreword

One brisk and cheery May morning, Stan Laurel — also feeling brisk and cheery — was answering a variety of questions from me about his films. During the course of this I turned unduly pedagogic (instinctively — I was then teaching Shakespeare at New York University), and I told Stan that as a team he and Oliver Hardy were patterned on the dumb servants of Roman comedy, a type brought to finest flower in some of Shakespeare's comics, notably Dogberry, Bottom and Sir Andrew Aguecheek.

In saying all this to Stan I was rather solemn about it. He looked at me even more solemnly and said, "Oh? I thought we were patterned after the Katzenjammer Kids!" before breaking into his lovely, very refined horse laugh.

I soon learned never to get too solemn with Stan and I also discovered that though he was the chief creative force of the team, he disliked talking about comedy theory in general and any analysis of his work in particular. The gags, yes. He loved to talk about them, but not about their meaning for the very good reason that he thought they had no meaning. "Don't ever ask me what comedy is or what makes people laugh," he said. "I don't know, and I bet sure as hell no one else knows either."

In essence, surely Stan was right. No one has ever satisfactorily explained what laughter is, and at the rate we are going, no one likely ever will.

Having said that, I think Stan would find in Mr. Nollen's work at hand some particular things of interest. Some not. The concept of Stan and Ollie, for instance, having enough character *as* characters to warrant psychological profiles is a thing I'm sure he'd deny. But I believe Stan would easily be caught up in the connection women had with his comedy. Women always fascinated him—perhaps because he had so little luck with them until the last 20 years of his life when he discovered the perfect wife in Ida Kitaeva.

What Stan probably least understood about his comedy was its unique extensions into the psyches of other people. The identity of Laurel and Hardy is certainly a various one in the bosoms of its beholders, and it is hardly surprising that comedy-questing people like Mr. Nollen would attempt to define that identity. There is not much doubt that identity search is the intellectual odyssey of our age, and it is inevitable that Laurel and Hardy should be a subject of it.

Yet I must present Stan's strongly held opinion that looking for any social or psychological rationale for the existence, continuing popularity and universality of Stan and Ollie is a fruitless search. For him the two existed purely and only to give laughter to the world.

To give Mr. Nollen credit he does not unduly belabor this business of finding a social rationale for his subjects, and I think he believes in entertainment as the basic reason for Stan and Ollie's existence. Stan certainly believed in it, passionately. He thought good comedy was shaped for only one purpose—laughter—and that adding social comment to it or finding social comment *in* it was not only pointless but pretty funny in the bargain.

I was his guest once when another comedy giant—who shared his convictions—dropped by to visit. Buster Keaton disliked the searching for and labeling of comedy structure. As they began to talk about their past, the subject of reading social comment into their films came up. That actively exasperated Buster. "When in the name of Christ," he said, "will these people learn that what we did was gags, gags, gags, and then more gags, and nothing more than gags, set inside a pleasant little story?" What indeed.

You will find ample labeling in what follows, heaven knows, but I think the reader will also find in Mr. Nollen's work some sound reflection and a consistent search for truth, all of this—I am glad to see—set warmly within a pervasive and understanding love of the greatest comedy team in history.

John McCabe
Mackinac Island, Michigan
April 1988

Table of Contents

Preface

This book is not a biographical text of the lives of Stan Laurel and Oliver Hardy or an exhaustive production history of their motion pictures. That information is available in other sources, many of which are mentioned in Chapter I. However, the book *is* a critical analysis of the work of Laurel and Hardy, with biographical and production information included when it pertains to film content.

A major critical approach does not dominate the material in this work. In order to present a comprehensive analysis, many critical disciplines, including an historical overview, textual analysis, the auteur theory, genre analysis, psychoanalytic theory, and theory of film technique and structure, have been used. The main purpose of this text is to provide a survey of the cinematic techniques and the thematics of the Laurel and Hardy films. Certain motifs are discussed at length, with minor conclusions provided where they appear to be applicable. This author demonstrates no definitive analytical conclusions, since this attitude, if at all possible, can certainly lead one into a "nice mess" indeed. I leave this realm open to the choice of each individual reader and film viewer.

When the real Stan Laurel and Oliver Hardy are mentioned in the text, they are referred to as "Laurel" and "Hardy." Their cinematic characters are called "Stan" and "Ollie" or "the Boys." The screen personas that these two men created are given the most consideration, since their performing styles and personal lives have been elucidated so well by past authors.

I believe that certain new approaches to the Laurel and Hardy films may be found in this text, and, hopefully, these are presented with enough filmic evidence to make them seem probable. Instead of merely discussing the comedy techniques in the films, I have attempted to analyze the team's work with respect to the structure and thematics of classic Hollywood film as a whole.

I would like to graciously thank John McCabe for writing the foreword to this volume. McCabe, who has had the advantage of knowing both Stan Laurel and Oliver Hardy, offers some interesting ideas on the *intent* of the artists responsible for creating the subject of this text. He also offered valuable assistance in clearing up some of the "red tape" I encountered prior to publication.

I would also like to thank my wife, Karla, for watching countless films, listening to my ideas about comedy, and putting up with me when I act like Stan Laurel and Oliver Hardy; Craig Nance, a Laurel and Hardy fanatic, who joined me in several marathon film viewings and helped to increase my appreciation of the team; Bart Aikens, who so diligently proofread the manuscript and curtailed my habit of using too many hyphens; Pat Byrnes, for his steadfast assistance at the copy machine; and my father, Harold N. Nollen, whose lifelong love of comedy films helped to create my initial interest in the subject.

Finally, I would like to extend my appreciation to the following individuals and organizations, who either aided my progress, provided encouragement, located film prints or illustrative material, joined me (willingly or not) in screening the films, or merely offered to lend their assistance: American Film Stars, Richard W. Bann, Ryan Baumbach, Eddie Brandt's Saturday Matinee, Nathan Brown, Jim Ennis, Helen and Earl Fischer, Robert Gossman, Rick Greene, Sir Alec Guinness, Lois Laurel Hawes, Todd "Dane" Jacobsen, John Jensen, the late Edward Lowry, Milton T. Moore, Corey Nelson, Shirley Nollen, Jerry Ohlinger's Movie Material Store, D. Lucas Skahill, John Soister, the Sons of the Desert, Duane Straight, Sgt. Jay F. Tiarks, and the University of Iowa Main Library.

Scott Allen Nollen
Iowa City, Iowa
May 1989

I.

Why Take
Laurel and Hardy Seriously?

"Remember how dumb I used to be? Well,
I'm better now."—Stan, *Block-Heads* (1938)

"[N]o one in films has been loved so universally and for so long as Laurel and Hardy," states Charles Barr in his 1967 book, *Laurel and Hardy*.[1] This statement perfectly describes the status of Stan Laurel and Oliver Hardy as popular screen comics—a comedy team admired by film buffs, but consistently neglected by film scholars. For many years, myths and biases have been created by cinema critics and theorists who have championed the works of comedians such as Charles Chaplin, Buster Keaton, and the Marx Brothers, but have largely ignored, or have dismissed as "low comedy," the work of Laurel and Hardy. Their films have often been referred to as simple works of slapstick, a superficial analysis that completely disregards the complex psychology of their unique characterizations.

Perhaps another reason for the disinterest of scholarly writers lies in the fact that the Laurel and Hardy films were not made to be taken seriously—an aspect that Stan Laurel took pains to stress whenever he was queried about the social content of comedy films. Why then, take Laurel and Hardy seriously? The question is multifaceted, drawing into consideration many aspects of the Laurel and Hardy cinematic world—aspects that are discussed in detail in the pages that follow. Much of what is to be learned about Laurel and Hardy is derived from an examination of their films and a comparison between the functioning of this team and other comedy performers.

Much like the comedy of Charles Chaplin, the Laurel and

1

Hardy comic world concerns itself with the intricacies and unpredictability of human behavior. All of the best Laurel and Hardy comedies deal with the relationship of two characters, Stan and Ollie, and the consequences of this undeniably unique pairing. Both Stan and Ollie possess their own set of bizarre personality traits and the plot of each film usually centers on an event in which these two personalities are combined. A typical result of this interaction is a conflict of some kind, sometimes between the two, but more often against some third party, usually resulting in an anarchic conclusion.

The combination of the two characters' actions, however, sets the Laurel and Hardy films apart from those of someone like Chaplin. Although Chaplin's films include inevitable conflicts, it is usually only Charlie who experiences the major effects of them. The Tramp is essentially a loner, an independent force, who sometimes becomes involved with another character, usually a pretty heroine. The Laurel and Hardy world is always dependent upon the actions of both Stan and Ollie, and this combination was the first of its kind to emerge in the comedy genre of the classic Hollywood cinema. The idea of comic partnership has existed for centuries, and many cinematic clowns, including Keaton, frequently worked with an on-screen partner, but Laurel and Hardy were the first well-developed comedy team to appear on the motion picture screen.

Unlike later comedy teams, Laurel and Hardy do not merely interact with one another, but exist as a unit. The Marx Brothers provide an interesting contrast to Laurel and Hardy, since they almost always function separately, depending on individual doses of verbal humor, or sometimes visual, in the case of Harpo. But the Marxes are hardly ever dependent upon one another—the rare incidents in which they do interact usually involve Chico laying the foundation for one of Groucho's punchlines. In the Laurel and Hardy films, Stan cannot effectively function without Ollie to tell him what to do, and Ollie cannot get anything done without Stan. On the other hand, as a unit, they never actually accomplish anything. If they do manage to see a task to completion, it is usually destroyed before the final fade out. But, unlike the Marx Brothers, Stan and Ollie share equally in their accomplishments *and* their failures.

The Stan and Ollie characters are not one-dimensional clowns like Abbott and Costello or the Three Stooges (teams which Laurel and Hardy have been compared to), but are richly textured individuals with fully developed psychological personas. These two childlike men tell us much about the nature of human beings in general, and perhaps constitute the most complex and bizarre couple to ever inhabit the Hollywood cinema.

Criticism of the work of Laurel and Hardy has never been particularly positive, or very good. On initial release, most of their films were either dismissed without being reviewed, or, at best, were mentioned in a few terse paragraphs in the review sections of the *New York Times* or *Variety*. Many essays from the early 1930s appear as if the author had not even seen the film in question, since plot lines and personnel are frequently attributed to the wrong film title.

Most reviewers referred to Laurel and Hardy with terms such as "buffoons" or "comics who display dry and bland shenanigans," as did Bosley Crowther in 1939.[2] Considering that, at that time, most film criticism was concerned with plot development and story elements, it is not surprising that most critics saw Laurel and Hardy in this light. A viewer does not have to see many of their films to realize that they were concerned with character and not plot. When plot is emphasized in the narrative, the aspects of their complex psychological personas almost always suffer.

There were, however, some critics of the 1930s who thought highly of Laurel and Hardy. Pare Lorentz, writing in *Judge* in 1930, states that "without a doubt, the two-reel comedies of Laurel and Hardy are the best directed and funniest movies being made today."[3] The word Lorentz uses is "funny," a word that perfectly describes an obvious aspect of the work of Laurel and Hardy, but falls far short of considering the complex essence and importance of their films as cultural artifacts.

The first book-length essay written about the team was John McCabe's *Mr. Laurel and Mr. Hardy,* first published in 1961. In the work, McCabe focuses on the personal lives, partnership, and comedy technique of Stan Laurel and Oliver Hardy. Charles Barr's 1967 book provides many interesting analytical insights about the characters of Stan and Ollie, but is fairly brief and only touches upon subjects that need to be discussed in greater detail. William K. Everson's *The Films of Laurel and Hardy,* also published in 1967, contains a large amount of erroneous information concerning film content and very little critical commentary.

A revival of interest in the comedy team prompted the release of Randy Skretvedt's *Laurel and Hardy: The Magic Behind the Movies* (1987), a meticulously researched volume which covers the production histories of each of the Laurel and Hardy films. Skretvedt spent seven years writing the work , interviewing many individuals who actually participated in the production of the films. The book is certainly written with Laurel and Hardy fans in mind, concentrating on what is *not* featured in the films (deleted sequences or scripted material that was not filmed), and providing a look at how the team actually controlled the creative process.

The most important aspect of the Laurel and Hardy method that has been ignored by criticism is its overall structure and content, which differs considerably from that of other comic performers and filmmakers. Scholarly criticism has predominantly considered the work of those who seem to have a concrete *purpose* in their comedy.

Charles Chaplin has been called "the greatest film artist in motion picture history."[4] This statement undoubtedly comes from an appreciation of Chaplin as an artist who has depicted the weaknesses and strengths of human relationships and human society. The Laurel and Hardy films also accomplish this task, but on a more self-effacing level.

Chaplin was conscious of every minute aspect of his films, openly choosing to include social commentary throughout his work. Not only did he choose to present a picture of society, but included heavy doses of self-glorification in the process. Chaplin is candid about this aspect of his work, as one reading of his *My Autobiography* (1964) reveals. The technique of Chaplin, although phenomenal in execution, is always obvious to the viewer, many times operating on a self-serving level. An incident in Chaplin's 1915 short, *The Pawn Shop,* provides an excellent example: while the Little Tramp is cleaning up a storeroom, he stops to walk, like a tightrope walker, on a piece of string which is stretched across the floor. Here, as in numerous other Chaplin films, the Tramp falls completely out of character, simply becoming Chaplin, the pantomimic artist (often shown in lovingly lingering close-ups). Chaplin's films usually conclude with the Tramp emerging triumphant, either winning the girl (in almost all of his work) or reaching truly heroic proportions (*Shoulder Arms,* 1918, and *The Great Dictator,* 1940). Stan and Ollie, however, rarely experience even marginal success in their exploits, and are usually worse off at film's end.

In the Chaplin films, Chaplin the actor, the director, the writer, and the composer of music is always noticeable. In contrast to this type of conscious narcissism, the Laurel and Hardy technique is seamless, almost unconscious. While on screen, Stan Laurel and Oliver Hardy are the characters of "Stan" and "Ollie," operating within their own surreal world. Their performance technique, especially that of Laurel, is subtle and unobtrusive, and is always coupled with an exquisite sense of timing. On this aspect, comedian Dick Van Dyke has commented:

> I consider Stan the greatest of film comedians. The reason is a very simple one. First of all because he got more laughs, both as a performer and as a creator of gags, than almost anyone else in film comedy. Not even Chaplin gets as much laughter, pure *laughter,* as Stan does. Chaplin is great — a genius — but with Chaplin I can always see the technique showing. Lord knows it's great technique, and I admire it very much — but with Stan the technique never shows. *Never.* And that to me is proof that he is a better craftsman than Chaplin — an infinitely better craftsman.[5]

The Laurel and Hardy films, like those of Chaplin, also comment on various sociocultural constructs, but do so in a way that lacks pretension. Chaplin's comedy, at times, reaches a level of direct address, with the content often becoming blatantly propagandistic (as in the final scene of *The Great Dictator*). According to Stan Laurel, he, Hardy, and his writers and directors, never consciously chose to include commentary, but it is present in many of the films, something that is analogous to Laurel's personal performing style — invisible intent with a visible result. With Chaplin, the viewer receives both food for thought and manipulative techique. On the other hand, the Laurel and Hardy world, although on a surreal plane of its own, indirectly comments on the real world.

This lack of pretension in the Laurel and Hardy films may account for the disinterest of past critics and scholars. Not much has been said about Laurel and Hardy, because, frankly, no "serious" film scholar has paid much attention to them. Discovering the richness of Laurel and Hardy does not involve exaggeration of the social aspects, or reading content into the narrative. That content is part of the film text, requiring a very observant and careful examination of all of these works.

Not only did Stan Laurel disapprove of using the comedy film as a vehicle for social commentary, but he also expressed contempt for film analysis. In a 1961 interview with John McCabe, he stated:

> That kind of junk annoys the hell out of me. What people like that don't understand and never will understand is that what we were trying to do was to make people laugh in as many ways as we could, without trying to prove a point or show the world its troubles or get into some deep meaning. Why the hell do you have to explain why a thing is funny? We were trying to do a very simple thing, give people some laughs, and that's *all* we were trying to do.
>
> If you think for one minute that Charlie [Chaplin] ever sat down and thought to himself, "Ah, ha! This is going to tell what's wrong with society!" you're wrong. He sat down to make people laugh and that's *all* he did. Just like me, Charlie's no intellectual, you know, no matter how brilliant he is — and in my opinion *no* one is more brilliant than Charlie — at making people *laugh*. That was his job; that was my job, and that's all we were good for. Charlie and Buster and Harry Langdon, Fields, and us — we were just doing as many good gags as we could. We weren't trying to change the world, or what the hell have you.
>
> Anyone who thinks *Modern Times* has got a big message is just putting it there himself. Charlie knew that the pressures of modern life and factory life would be good for a lot of *laughs,* and that's why he did the film — not because he wanted to diagnose the industrial revolution or some goddamned thing.[6]

It is apparent from these statements that Stan Laurel seriously underestimated, or simply did not care much about, the scope and power of screen comedy. Whenever a film, dramatic or comic, is produced within a particular culture, there are many endemic social values and practices which "find their way" into the work. In the case of Chaplin, it has been noted that most of his social references were completely intentional. Stan Laurel and others who worked on the Laurel and Hardy films may not have intended to include certain incidents in the film content, but that content is apparent, nonetheless. Evidently, Laurel did not choose to utilize specific psychological or value-oriented material; rather, it exists on a more *subconscious* level. Why certain things appear funny to people is one of the many complexities of human behavior, and, in the world of comedy, laughter is usually provoked by nothing less than human failure, stupidity, and suffering.

By making comedy films, Laurel and Hardy hoped to provide laughter for film audiences. They certainly attained this goal, but they also accomplished much more than that. By *not* intending to do so, they also created a coherent statement about human relationships and society.

II.
Stan Laurel

"Stan was the greatest. Even greater
than Chaplin. Charlie was second.
And don't let anyone fool you about
that." — Buster Keaton, to Andy Clyde
(February 26, 1965)[1]

Stan Laurel (born Arthur Stanley Jefferson at Ulverston, England, on June 16, 1890) acquired early training from his father, Arthur J. Jefferson. "Jeff" was an actor-writer-director in the English theatre, and frequently allowed his son to observe his work from backstage. From an early age, young Jefferson was particularly interested in comedy and idolized the great English music hall comic Dan Leno. In 1906, he formed his own small comedy revue, and a short time later joined Fred Karno's comedy troupe, which included another young comic named Charles Chaplin. His experiences with the Karno company proved to be invaluable, as he became exposed to the workings and the classic comedy technique of the music hall, allowing him to acquire the same basic training as Chaplin.

In 1910, Jefferson traveled to the United States with Karno, acting as Chaplin's understudy in the classic *A Night in an English Music Hall*. Karno worked the American vaudeville circuit, which was still a lucrative outlet, not yet challenged by the success of Hollywood film product. In 1913, Chaplin left the company to begin appearing in films for Mack Sennett, allowing Jefferson to fill his role as a drunk in the Karno production. Jefferson performed a superb imitation of Chaplin onstage, but Karno's American booking company insisted that the "real" Charles Chaplin was contracted to essay the role. A short time later, Jefferson was fired, leaving him to seek other work in the American vaudeville industry. Teaming up with other Karno refugees, he acted in various comedy productions,

9

frequently impersonating Chaplin, but constantly refining his abilities as mime and gag writer.

In 1917, Jefferson (changing his name to Stan Laurel) acted in his first Hollywood motion picture, appearing in approximately 75 films before teaming with Oliver Hardy in 1926. Laurel's early films are an extremely uneven mixture of slapstick and strange sight gags. His first major productions were made at Universal Studios, where he was contracted to play the lead character in the "Hickory Hiram" series. Most of these films are quite unremarkable, with Laurel basically depending upon Sennett-style physical comedy.

Laurel first met Hal Roach in 1918, obtaining a contract to star in a short series of one-reelers. Only modestly popular, the films did not bring him much artistic or financial success, and he found work very hard to come by until Roach signed him for a second series of films in 1923. The most accessible of Laurel's early films, this series includes many gags that he would later rework into the Laurel and Hardy films. But, unlike his later work, these films include breakneck pacing, with as many gags as could possibly be inserted into a ten-minute running time.

Laurel's acting style during this period is almost completely different than his later Stan character. Instead of utilizing subtle expression, curiosity, and pathos, Laurel relies on a more exaggerated technique, which includes a frantic dancing motion and a wide-eyed toothy smile, which he never uses when appearing with Oliver Hardy. Most of the Roach films are broad parodies of then-popular dramatic films, and include *Under Two Jags, Frozen Hearts,* and *The Soilers* (all 1923).

George Stevens, who served as cinematographer on 27 of the Laurel and Hardy projects, and later would become one of the finest of all American filmmakers, once commented on the early Laurel technique:

> Some time before beginning at Roach, I had seen Stan work, and I thought he was one of the unfunniest comedians around. He wore his hair in a high pompadour and usually played a congenital dude or slicker. He laughed and smiled too much as a comedian. He needed and wanted laughs, so much that he made a habit of laughing at himself as a player, which is extremely poor comic technique. How he changed! In those early days he was obviously searching for a formula.[2]

Early in his film career, Laurel appeared with Oliver Hardy in *Lucky Dog* (1919). The two encounter each other in one brief scene, with Laurel as the star and Hardy executing a secondary role. Laurel's second collaboration with Hardy came in 1925, when he directed Hardy in *Wandering Papas* for Roach. The following year, the two crossed paths again when Laurel was asked to fill in for Hardy in *Get 'Em Young*. Although Roach had agreed to give Laurel a position as writer and director, he was asked to essay Hardy's role, after Hardy scalded his arm with fat while basting a leg of lamb. Later, Laurel would comment that *Get 'Em Young* allowed him to create part of the Stan character, as he does a good deal of whimpering while on-screen.[3]

Many of Laurel's films of the 1920s are not very good, featuring only a very loosely connected string of gags, many of which are brilliant in conception, but poor in execution. One of the main reasons for this was the rushed production schedule and low budgets that Laurel and his directors faced during this period, with some films being completed in only a few days. *West of Hot Dog* (1924), a film made by the Joe Rock Company, is a good example of a bad Stan Laurel film. Laurel plays a western hero who spends an entire two reels rounding up a gang of extremely ineffectual bandits. His acting in this film is so ridiculous that it is difficult to believe that it is the same Stan Laurel who, less than three years later, would develop into the fine actor and writer of the Laurel and Hardy films.

There are, however, some character traits that Laurel developed in these early films that he would use later with Oliver Hardy. The trademark double take, which he would hone to absolute perfection in 1929–30, and the skip (jumping straight into the air with one leg thrust forward and the other thrust backward), a technique used frequently in the Laurel and Hardy film *Putting Pants on Philip* (1927), are used in several of the films. His character's relation to physical objects is also somewhat similar to that of the later Stan, since he is consistently unable to complete a mechanical task, such as loading lumber in *The Noon Whistle* (1923), sorting fruit in *Oranges and Lemons* (1923), or fishing in *Save the Ship* (1923).

One character trait that Laurel frequently exhibits in early films is a penchant for pursuing beautiful young women (something that most comics of the era did with a passion). A 1918 Roach film,

Just Rambling Along, features Laurel harassing an innocent female, while attempting to obtain a free meal. Set in a café, the film is a perverse imitation of Chaplin's *The Immigrant* (1917). Particularly in the Roach films of 1923, his character openly chases and aggravates female characters, notably in *Kill or Cure* (1923) and *A Man About Town* (1923). He rarely uses this strategy in the early Laurel and Hardy films (*Putting Pants on Philip* is one of the few).

The most important aspect of Stan Laurel's career at this time was his opportunity to experiment with gag writing and execution. He appeared in a sufficient number of films and was given enough space to function as writer and director to allow him to develop ideas for techniques and structures that he would soon employ in many superb Laurel and Hardy shorts. His experiences both in front of and behind the camera allowed him to develop an understanding of all aspects of the cinematic process, most importantly a knowledge of the shot and the strategies of editing (for both continuity and timing).

Laurel always attempted to work closely with the director, and, in all of the later Laurel and Hardy films, insisted on shooting the films in sequence to insure a smooth progression from one incident to the next. Laurel devised many story outlines, situations, and gags, and, along with Hal Roach, had control over the final cut of each film. An extremely modest filmmaker, he is never mentioned as a technician in the on-screen credits.

One of Stan Laurel's main contributions to film structure was his work during the post-production process. Working closely with the head editor Richard Currier and his assistant, Bert Jordan, Laurel personally supervised the cutting of all the Laurel and Hardy films from 1927 to 1940. All of the best Laurel and Hardy films feature a deliberately relaxed, constant tempo, a feature which helps to sustain atmosphere as well as contributing an element of subtlety to the frequently chaotic proceedings. Laurel created this tempo by using a technique which he called "holding," or timing the laughs of an audience at a sneak preview of one of his films. By doing this, he could determine how long to hold a particular shot before cutting to the next. In *Mr. Laurel and Mr. Hardy,* John McCabe states that Laurel felt that "his earlier directors took the pictures along at too great a speed. He discussed the idea of 'holding' with [Clyde] Bruckman and other directors."[4]

In 1926, Stan Laurel had been in the motion picture business for nine years, experiencing only marginal success as a comedy actor, writer, and director. Developing a knowledge of the structure of comic situations and a penchant for mime, he needed only one thing to bring his talent to fruition: Oliver Hardy.

The partnership with Oliver Hardy and the amount of creative freedom afforded by Hal Roach gave Stan Laurel the ability to develop a style which has no equal in the comedy cinema. Comments made by the late George Stevens again provide a vivid description:

> As to their work together, Stan was the story man, Babe [Hardy] was the golfer, and Babe liked it that way. One day I walked into the projection room at Roach's, and Stan was the only one there. He was watching some Laurel and Hardy rushes, and as he watched, he howled with laughter. I recall his feet were in the air; he was bicycling them furiously in a reaction of utter merriment. He knew what was good; there was no need for fake modesty. He laughed especially at Babe, and that not only because Babe was such a superb comedian but because Stan had the chance that creative people get so rarely — of seeing his own ideas not only brought to life but brought to life more magnificently than he had ever dared to dream they would be.[5]

III.
Oliver Hardy

Hardy, "the fat one," was perhaps
less creative than his partner ... but
his comic characterizations were superb,
and he made the most of his bulky figure,
cherubic face, and expressive eyes to
bring hours of laughter to millions.[1]
—Ephraim Katz (1979)

Norvell Hardy was born in Harlem, Georgia, on January 18, 1892. His father, Oliver Hardy, a successful lawyer and politician, died when Hardy was a small child. Shortly thereafter, his mother, forced to seek a profession of her own, purchased a hotel and moved the family to Madison, Georgia. It was in Madison that Hardy first became interested in acting. While sitting in his mother's hotel, he became fascinated with how people behaved as they entered the lobby.

Changing his name to Oliver Norvell Hardy, in memory of his father, Hardy joined his first entertainment troupe at the age of eight. Singing soprano with the group, he became interested in music and decided that he would dedicate his life to it. Already weighing in at two hundred and fifty pounds at the age of 14, Hardy decided to study voice at the Atlanta Conservatory of Music. This desire did not last very long, however, and he later entered the University of Georgia in order to study law. Again, Hardy was not pleased with his choice of vocation, and after moving to Milledgeville with his family in 1910, he opened a motion picture theatre in the small Georgia town.

Films began to interest Hardy at this point, and he became particularly fond of two-reel comedies, which were shown regularly at the theatre. By 1913, he could stand the business no longer, and decided to move to Jacksonville, Florida, to join the Lubin film

15

company. First working as a prop boy and assistant, he soon found his way into small acting parts, and, a short time later, began playing "heavies" in comedy films. He appeared in approximately 50 films over the next five years, developing an acting style that has many similarities to his later "Ollie" character. The Oliver Hardy of the Lubin films, like the Ollie of the Laurel and Hardy films, exhibits a distinct air of "Southern hospitality," as Hardy referred to it. In many of the films, he appears as the somewhat fumbling, but always courteous and polite, gentleman.

In *Hungry Hearts* (1916), he portrays a painter who falls in love with his subject. He is unsuccessful in courting the rich widow, as his sly business partner marries her first, in order to appropriate all of her money. The character in this film is very similar to the Ollie character, in that he becomes infatuated with a woman, only to experience rejection for his efforts. Much more than the Stan character, Ollie is always interested in the opposite sex, but in a naive, childlike manner.

In 1917, Hardy moved to California in order to appear in films for Mack Sennett, Hal Roach, and others. He starred in several shorts with Larry Semon, Jimmy Aubrey, and Billy West, who became the most famous of the Charles Chaplin imitators working in Hollywood. Prior to his teaming with Stan Laurel in 1926, Hardy appeared in over 200 films. Unlike Laurel, he also appeared in a few films after their partnership was formed (several in 1927–28, one in 1939, one in 1949, and one in 1950).

Some of Hardy's films are quite good, particularly a short series of two-reelers in which he supported Bobby Ray, a comic who has long since been forgotten. Produced by Billy West in 1925, these films possess what could be called the germ of Laurel and Hardy. In a 1954 interview with John McCabe, Hardy commented on one of the films, *Stick Around:*

> . . . [T]here was one picture I made in 1925 that seemed to have some kind of tie-in with the pictures I made with Stan later. The picture was one called *Stick Around.* I barely knew Stan at this time, and us as a team was still in the future. And yet this picture, in a way, was like a Laurel and Hardy comedy. I made the picture with Bobby Ray, who was a slight man, on the short side. Didn't look like Stan but he was an opposite to me. I'll tell you what I can remember about the plot. We were paperhangers; I was the boss, Bobby was my helper. I was always giving him orders and he was always getting the short

end of the stick. I remember we were walking up a hill. He was pulling our cart loaded with wallpaper. I wasn't doing my work naturally. We get to the top and I tell him we're on the wrong street. He lets the wagon fly back down the hill and then it gets mixed up with a wagon that has a lot of circus posters on it. We reclaim our wagon and go over to the job we're working on which is a hospital. So, as you can imagine, the rest of the picture is full of stuff about getting circus billboards mixed up with the regular paper and all that. Bobby always played the fall guy; I was the wise guy just as I am in Laurel and Hardy, only in Laurel and Hardy, I always am the fall guy. I think of that picture once in a while as being the start of the Laurel and Hardy idea as far as I was concerned.[2]

Traditionally, critics who have written about Laurel and Hardy have given almost all of the auteur credit to Stan Laurel (along with Leo McCarey and Hal Roach, who originally paired the two men). It is true that Laurel wrote and directed parts of many of the films, but the Bobby Ray films present Oliver Hardy in an interesting light. The team idea does appear to come from Hardy's earlier films, and not from Laurel's. Although Hardy expressed no interest in writing or direction, preferring instead to remain an actor, he may have subconsciously created more of Laurel and Hardy than he realized. *Stick Around* is basically a Laurel and Hardy film without Laurel although Bobby Ray is in no way comparable to Laurel as a performer). There is a memorable sequence in the film in which Hardy first scolds the bumbling Ray, and then forgives him. Much like Laurel and Hardy, there is a touching scene with Ray telling Hardy that he loves him, kissing him on the head.

Another Ray film, *Hop to It* (1925), features a mixture of Hardy's various cinematic personas. He and Ray play bellhops at a big city hotel who both attempt to rob one of the guests of his large money bag, causing a frantic chase in the Sennett style (something that was used very seldom in the Laurel and Hardy films). Ray and Hardy appear in scenes together, but only act as a team in a few short sequences. Hardy's character is a combination of his *Stick Around* paperhanger and his earlier heavy roles. This film was released just before *Stick Around,* providing a look at the development of Hardy's Ollie-type persona.

By 1925, the seed had been planted for the Ollie character, but it would take a few films with Stan Laurel to bring out the well-known Ollie mannerisms: the fumbling with his hands and necktie, the painful gaze into the camera, and the paralanguage that can be witnessed throughout the films (the singing, humming, and disgusted grunts that he issues toward Stan). Oliver Hardy would continue to develop this fascinating character over the next 14 years, in some of the finest screen comedies of the 1920s and 1930s.

IV.
Cinematic and Comic Structure

"Mr. Laurel says, that after viewing the
situation from all sides, he is thoroughly
reconciled to the fact that the moving-
picture industry is still in its infancy."
—radio announcer, *Me and My Pal* (1933)

Structurally, the Laurel and Hardy shorts and features from
1926 to 1940 maintain a simple and consistent style. John McCabe
has pointed out that "it was not easy to incorporate novelty at
every turn when one is expected to complete ten two-reel films
a year."[1] However, much of the content presented within this
cinematic framework is quite complex, both physically and psychologically.

The world of Laurel and Hardy incorporates many centuries
of comedy technique and style, but most notably is derived from
the pantomime and structuring techniques of the English music
hall. The films, like most classic comedies, consist of a well-timed
series of gags, but Laurel and Hardy add something to this well-
established form: complex characterization. Other comics before
them had done this—Chaplin's tramp is a real character, but is essentially somewhat static and predictable, and some of Keaton's
characters, amazing though they are, usually exist only to triumph
over various physical obstacles (both always appear to be the unlikely comic hero).

The plots of the Laurel and Hardy films usually consist of a
loosely defined conflict, either between Stan and Ollie, or between
them as a team and another party. Unlike the members of other motion picture comedy teams, neither Laurel nor Hardy can be considered a straight man or a fall guy. In most of their films, each incorporates qualities of both types of characters, constantly playing off
each other or the third party.

19

There are a great number of gag motifs used throughout the films, the content being a direct result of the personalities of the two characters. Other than "single" gag strategies (a comic incident used only once in a film), Laurel and Hardy created two specific gag structures, which Charles Barr describes as the "triple gag" and the "open-ended gag."[2]

The triple gag consists of a certain action repeated three times within the same scene or narrative. *The Finishing Touch* (1928) features Ollie swallowing an entire handful of nails at three different times, never learning his lesson between incidents. A film made that same year, *From Soup to Nuts,* again has Ollie making the same mistake thrice, this time falling into a large cake while attempting to serve it to high-class guests. Incidents such as these appear throughout the films, usually featuring Ollie being careless or Stan aiding him in his stupidity.

The open-ended gag is the form most associated with Laurel and Hardy, and has also been referred to as the tit for tat routine or the act of reciprocal destruction. Films which feature the tit for tat form usually begin with Stan and Ollie innocently attempting to complete a task. Such everyday events as driving, walking down a street, playing a musical instrument, or offering a product to a prospective customer typically result in a scene of methodically constructed chaos, with huge crowds of people joining in the violence and destruction. Although many of these scenes seem senselessly violent, the viewer is always encouraged to laugh in the face of near-annihilation. The most bizarre aspect of this tit for tat technique is that all characters involved always politely wait for the next atrocity to be committed, either to themselves or to their property.

The first of the great chaotic films, *Hats Off* (1927), features a crowd of townspeople engaging in a massive battle, with individuals destroying each other's headgear. Last seen in its original release, *Hats Off* has been a lost film for 60 years.

The Battle of the Century (1927) features the most colossal pie fight to appear in any classic comedy. The battle begins when Ollie's banana peel causes a pie vendor to slip and then retaliate by splattering Ollie with a pie. Stan hands Ollie some pies from the vendor's truck, and soon, all hell breaks loose, with many bystanders joining in the escalating skirmish.

Shortly before production of *The Battle of the Century,* Stan

Laurel explained his reasoning behind the use of the open-ended routine: "Look, if we make a pie picture—let's make a pie picture to end all pie pictures. Let's give them so many pies that there will never be room for any more pie pictures in the whole history of the movies."[3] Variations on this film include *Should Married Men Go Home?* (1928), which substitutes mud for pies, and *The Hoose-Gow* (1929), featuring a rice-throwing contest between Stan and Ollie, a group of convicts, and some politicians.

In *You're Darn Tootin'* (1928), Stan and Ollie, standing in front of a restaurant, start a fight that eventually involves the whole of the surrounding community. Bellies are punched, shins are kicked, clothing is shredded and thrown into the air, but after one character commits an act, he waits for another to be done to himself before he continues in the battle.

Two Tars (1928) features scenes of many citizens involved in disassembling each other's automobiles, culminating in a wild demolition derby. What first starts out as a traffic jam caused by road construction becomes total war after Stan and Ollie arrive in their Model T, obliviously driving to the front of the line.

Perhaps their best silent, *Big Business* (1929), features Stan and Ollie as Christmas tree salesmen who decide to peddle their wares in Southern California. After a homeowner (James Finlayson) refuses their offer, Stan starts an altercation by damaging some of the trim on his house. The homeowner retaliates by chopping up a Christmas tree, causing Ollie to destroy another household ornament. Destruction continues, always alternating between the two parties, until Stan and Ollie's car and the homeowner's dwelling are almost completely demolished. The 1935 short *Tit for Tat* is essentially a sound version of *Big Business,* with Charlie Hall playing a belligerent grocery store owner.

These scenes of destruction always end with Stan and Ollie apologizing and being absolved, calmly walking away, or a combination of the two. An air of consideration is always maintained between the two men and their rivals, something Raymond Durgnat has suggested is a character's "obedience to some strange relic from the Code of the West, perhaps deliberately stroking up his own indignation and therefore strength, perhaps out of bravado, perhaps out of obedience to some streak of masochism which, if Laurel and

Hardy films are any guide, must be more compulsive in human nature than common sense would have us believe."[4]

One of the most interesting aspects of the Laurel and Hardy films is the way in which the two characters' interpersonal space is constructed within the *mise-en-scène*. Most of the early films rely heavily upon the long take, a silent-era technique which was revived in the European cinema of the 1930s and '40s by filmmakers such as Jean Renoir and Roberto Rosselini, among many others. Chaplin, Keaton, and Lloyd were fond of using this technique, but the shots in their films predominantly feature one major character working within the frame. Laurel and Hardy take full advantage of the long take by actually *showing* the comic interactions that take place between Stan and Ollie. Many of their best films contain long-take scenes that feature realistic events — their on-screen actions are real to the viewer, since they are performed within a single shot and are not created by editing several different shots together.

The early silent shorts feature a decided "documentary impulse," showing Stan and Ollie interacting within actual exterior settings. Instead of constructing a desired location in the studio or on a backlot, as did Chaplin, these films continually feature the streets and buildings of Culver City, California (the town in which Roach Studios was located). Interiors of buildings, such as hotels and stores, are also frequently used as settings. Charles Barr has called Laurel and Hardy the comic equivalent of Alfred Hitchcock, stating that, no matter how outrageous their behavior may be, it retains a plausible atmosphere "from having its roots fixed in the ordinary."[5]

Putting Pants on Philip is a good example of surreal events depicted within a real setting. Hardy portrays Piedmont Mumblethunder, a respected citizen, who is embarrassed when he meets his nephew, Philip (Laurel), a kilted Scotsman, at the docks. The entire film consists of Mumblethunder's attempts to make Philip respectable by purchasing him a pair of trousers. Mumblethunder is also appalled by Philip's insane desire to chase attractive young women whenever he spots them on the street. Several scenes consist of a long shot in which a huge crowd forms around Philip as he tracks down a beautiful woman. There is an effect of deep focus in these shots, with Mumblethunder running from the foreground to the background of the frame, in an effort to stop Philip before it is too late. Shot on actual city streets, with throngs of spectators observing the antics of Mumblethunder and Philip, this film does seem undeniably real at times.

The Laurel and Hardy films which feature elements of chaos all contain long takes composed in depth. Scores of characters engaged in full-scale battles in such films as *The Battle of the Century, You're Darn Tootin',* and *Two Tars* can all be seen acting out their violent frustrations within a single shot. These battles take place in front of restaurants, shops, and businesses, or on country roads where men are attempting to work — always within the context of realistic, commonplace events.

Leave 'Em Laughing (1928), directed by Keaton associate Clyde Bruckman, features Stan and Ollie, under the influence of laughing gas, causing a huge traffic jam in the center of town. Shot on the main streets of Culver City, with the protagonists surrounded by ordinary people going about their mundane business, this film contains many moments of what Andre Bazin called "essential cinema."[6]

The most important aspect of the long take is that it allows Laurel and Hardy to perform *with* each other, using their sense of tempo instead of tightening actions with editing. Most of the silents are shot in this manner, but *Liberty* (1929) is possibly the best example. Involving escaped convicts Stan and Ollie attempting to elude the authorities, much of *Liberty* shows them atop an actual skyscraper structure, which was constructed on the roof of a 150-foot building in downtown Los Angeles. This film contains no backscreen or process shots, and the actions performed by Laurel and Hardy on the skyscraper are real. Many shots have a deep focus quality, with Stan and Ollie on a girder in the foreground and the high-rise buildings, billboards, and streets of Los Angeles behind and below them.

Charles Barr comments that "the whole skyscraper scene is superb, shot not only with exact timing but with such apparent authenticity as to communicate vertigo directly; but one can hardly overestimate the importance of a construction which makes the episode as probable, as normal, as anything in a neo-realist script."[7]

Wrong Again (1929) features some of the finest long-take gags in the Laurel and Hardy films. There are three shots, each lasting over a minute in length, in which Stan and Ollie attempt to

successfully place a live horse on top of a millionaire's piano (a parody of one of the scenes in the Luis Bunuel–Salvador Dali film *Un Chien Andalou* [1928]).

The first shot shows Stan examining a statue of a nude man that Ollie has broken and erroneously reassembled (the buttocks now face forward). Attempting to make sense of the strange image, Stan does nine subtle double takes within the single shot.

The second shot shows Stan and Ollie standing in front of the piano, with the horse standing on top of it. Pleased with their successful effort, they lean relaxedly up against the piano, as the animal begins to nuzzle Stan's hat. The horse knocks Stan's hat to the floor a total of six times. Thinking that Ollie is responsible, Stan tosses his partner's hat to the floor an equal number of times.

The third and final long-take scene has Ollie supporting the piano with his back while Stan attempts to put a wooden support back under it. Here, the horse knocks Stan's hat off ten more times, each time forcing him to leave Ollie to suffer while he retrieves it.

Several films use this technique to show progressive movement from foreground to background, with Ollie usually being overtaken by some powerful, heavy object. *Bacon Grabbers* (1929) features Ollie being dragged down a sidewalk by a large dog, and *The Music Box* (1932) has Ollie painfully pulled down a long flight of stairs by a piano. In these and the aforementioned shots, the camera remains static with all the movement created by on-screen characters and objects.

The Laurel and Hardy long-take does frequently include an unusual moving camera technique that is essentially a backward dolly motion (the kind of which D.W. Griffith was so fond). Their earliest films feature this technique, with *Putting Pants on Philip* again being a notable example. A dolly shot lasting one minute and ten seconds shows Mumblethunder and Philip walking down the sidewalk toward the camera. In an attempt to remain honorable, Mumblethunder attempts to stay several yards ahead of Philip, who is still wearing his garish kilt.

A hilarious version of this technique appears in *You're Darn Tootin'*, as Stan and Ollie walk down the middle of a street. Suddenly,

Opposite: Stan's maneuvering provides a temporary success for the Boys in *Wrong Again* (1929), one of the team's finest long-take comedies.

Stan completely drops out of the shot, while Ollie remains. The camera halts momentarily, and then dollies backward a few more feet. Stan's legs can then be seen sticking out of a manhole.

Liberty combines this movement with deep focus in a shot in which Stan and Ollie are being chased by a prison guard. The camera moves back at an incredible speed, with the "convicts" in the foreground and the guard far behind them.

The long take is used predominantly in the silent shorts, although it does appear in several of the later sound shorts and features, such as the aforementioned *The Music Box* and *The Fixer-Uppers* (1935), which contains one of the longest single takes in any of the Laurel and Hardy films. Their films are actually a conglomeration of many stylistic techniques, since many different directors and cinematographers worked with Laurel and Hardy throughout their filmmaking careers. During the transition from silent to sound films, some of their work became cramped and static, due to the microphone stranglehold, but soon after, their films began to combine the older, shot-in-depth technique with various editing strategies (with one style never completely overtaking the other).

Editing is used very sparingly, but occasionally a comic moment needs some degree of manipulation in order to function successfully, and this type of incident is usually alternated with long-take material. The best Laurel and Hardy films feature an exact, but relaxed, tempo, constructed of the team's precisely timed interactions in predominantly long takes, juxtaposed when editing is necessary. The Stan and Ollie interactions are rarely created by cutting, but, as in any film, the relationship between one incident and the next is formed by this process. Editing in the early silents is very simplistic, usually used to connect one scene to the next (with very little cutting within the scenes).

Occasionally, cutting will be used to add a moment of suspense, as in the final scene of *Do Detectives Think?* (1927), or to stress a running gag, such as a woman (Anita Garvin) attempting to corner a salad cherry in *From Soup to Nuts.* On those rare occasions when cross-cutting is used, it usually stresses the progression of an act that Stan and Ollie started earlier in the narrative, such as the train passengers' clothes-ripping tit for tat in *Berth Marks* (1929).

The most common type of dynamic editing in the films is the use of a cutaway, or reaction shot, that usually shows a bystander or crowd of people reacting to one of Stan and Ollie's absurd situations. This type of shot comprises the rare incidence when editing creates comic effect in the Laurel and Hardy films. When Stan's kilt flies up into the air (à la Marilyn Monroe) in *Putting Pants on Philip,* the scene cuts to a shot of women fainting (a previous shot has shown Stan losing his boxer shorts, hence the strong reaction). In *You're Darn Tootin',* one shot shows a pantsless fat man, jumping up and down, yelling, "I've been robbed." The next shot shows Stan and Ollie walking away from the scene, sharing the same huge pair of trousers.

Hog Wild (1930) includes one of Stan and Ollie's apocalyptic auto-destruction scenes, in which their Model T is demolished. Stan has driven the vehicle onto streetcar tracks and cannot get it restarted. Sounds of a streetcar can be heard behind them as the scene cuts to spectators, who cower away from the scene (as hideous demolition sounds are heard on the soundtrack). The scene then cuts back to the car, which has been crushed. Stan then starts the "redesigned" Model T and drives into the fade out. Here, the entire gag is created by cutting to another shot. The suspense of waiting to see what the damaged auto looks like creates viewer anticipation, and, most importantly, laughter.

Brats (1930) is a film that could not exist without a great deal of editing. Laurel and Hardy play themselves and their sons, who look exactly like their fathers (except for "little Ollie," who does not sport the Hardy mustache). The space between fathers and sons in *Brats* is created through editing, and, in the establishing shot, through superimposition. Two sizes of sets were built for this film, one normal size and the other in huge proportions, in order to make the two actors appear small enough to be children. Shots of the fathers are alternated with the sons, and, curiously enough, a reasonably realistic atmosphere is maintained throughout the film. A similar strategy is also used in *Twice Two* (1933), in which Laurel and Hardy portray themselves and their wives.

More editing is used in the sound films than in the silents, possibly due to the more difficult conditions imposed by the microphone. Working in the sound format, Laurel and Hardy not only had to sustain a lengthy routine visually, but aurally as well. Many gags which are depicted in a single shot in the silent films are presented in two separate shots in many of the sound films. The first shot usually shows one of the characters performing an action, while the second shows the effect of the previous action. In *Tit for Tat,* one scene features Stan hitting Mr. Hall (Charlie Hall) in the face with a spoonful of potato salad—the first shot showing Stan flinging it, the second showing the salad slapping Hall's face. In an earlier film, such as *Big Business,* this action probably would have been registered in a single take.

Close-ups are used sparingly, but very effectively, in all of the films. Some of the films include close-ups that introduce Stan and Ollie into an already established narrative. *The Battle of the Century* begins with a "world championship" boxing match. A minute or so into the film, the referee announces the name of the challenger, Canvasback Clump. The scene cuts to a close-up of Stan, who is sitting dazedly on a stool in his corner of the ring. This shot is possibly the funniest single shot of Stan Laurel ever used in a film. Close-ups of Ollie are usually utilized when he has just been through some horrible accident or subjected to some idiotic action of Stan's. These close-ups linger on the screen longer than any others and contain Ollie's frustrated gazes into the camera, tie-twiddling activities, or polite apologies to other characters.

Close-ups are used quite frequently in scenes which involve female characters. Whenever Stan and Ollie meet two women they are interested in, alternating shots of the men and the women are always used. *Their Purple Moment* (1928), *Two Tars,* and *The Devil's Brother* (1933) all contain this editing technique—Stan and Ollie make childlike facial expressions at the women and the women respond by registering coy looks back at them. These close-ups comprise some of the most bizarre moments in any of the films.

Alternating close-ups are also used to effectively separate Stan and Ollie from certain female characters, most notably their wives in *We Faw Down* (1929). The final scene of this film involves the two husbands attempting to explain what appeared to be an extramarital incident. Shots of the "guilty" men are juxtaposed with extreme close-ups of the angry females. This scene stresses the strong sense of isolation that Stan and Ollie are experiencing with their spouses.

Editing technique in the Laurel and Hardy films is uniformly good, with a very few exceptions. *Any Old Port* (1932) is a short that contains two parts—the main action of the piece, which involves Stan and Ollie as sailors, getting a room at an inn; and, later, a boxing match between Stan and Mugsie Long (Walter Long), owner of the inn. This latter sequence does not look like the rest of the film, and consists of a poorly shot sporting event made even worse by bad editing. A rehash of events from *Battle of the Century* and Chaplin's *City Lights* (1931), this scene shows Stan, in two static shots, running around the ring with Long chasing after him. The camera never moves, but remains fixed in a cramped medium shot, missing the action that is going on in the ring. This scene is the only incidence of its kind in their work, and one wonders why such an embarrassment was included in one of their films.

One other badly constructed scene appears in their work—the final sequence of *County Hospital* (1932). The most impressive visual element of their work, the "documentary impulse," is completely ignored in this scene, which involves a drugged Stan attempting to pilot his Model T. Instead of shooting live action in an actual city location, as was usually their method, they chose to utilize an inferior backscreen projection technique, with the Model T placed on a revolving pedestal. Not only does the projection look unrealistic, but all sense of proportion and perspective is lost, comprising a disappointing denouement to what, up until that moment, is an excellent Laurel and Hardy film. Evidently, location shooting was discouraged during this period, with Hal Roach Studios attempting to adjust to a depressed economy.

Several of the silent shorts utilize actual documentary footage as a prologue. This technique has the effect of creating a realistic atmosphere which is quickly subverted by cutting to an outrageous incident involving Stan and Ollie. *Two Tars* opens with footage of United States Navy troops and vessels. A title card states, "Two dreadnoughts from the B.S. Oregon," causing the scene to cut to Stan and Ollie, grinning from ear to ear, driving down the road in their Model T.

A similar scene appears at the beginning of *Liberty,* in which portraits of George Washington and Abraham Lincoln and footage of the First World War are included. The premise here is the continual democratic fight for liberty, with a title card stating, "And today, the fight for liberty continues." The next image is a shot of escapees Stan and Ollie being chased down a dirt road by a prison guard. What begins as a propagandistic message quickly turns into a Mack Sennett–style chase scene.

The coming of sound to the Laurel and Hardy films not only influenced editing strategies, but also added another dimension to the possibilities of their work. Unlike other comics who thrived in the silent era and either refused to work with dialogue (Chaplin) or became obsolete (Keaton, Langdon), Laurel and Hardy, along with W.C. Fields, became more successful because of the technology. The film-going public not only realized that Stan Laurel and Oliver Hardy were amazing pantomimists, but that they possessed fine speaking voices and acting abilities as well. Although they chose to utilize the many possibilities that sound film offered, they did not alter their comic style in the least. Laurel and Hardy still relied on visual technique, using dialogue only when necessary. In the words of John McCabe, "they utilized sound; they were not ruled by it."[8]

The relationship that exists between Stan and Ollie in the silent films becomes even more developed in the sound films. Stan adds a new dimension to his character—a penchant for butchering well-known English words, phrases, and clichés (something John McCabe calls the "rhetoric strangle"), a technique that would not have worked had the words been printed on title cards in silent films. Ollie also further develops his character, most notably adding a selection of sayings and disgusted sighs to his already established camera looks.

Sound afforded them the opportunity to actually speak the type of dialogue that they had already been using on title cards from 1927 to 1929. Since the team never relied on verbal jokes, but instead stressed the sight gag and unorthodox psychological behavior, their style made the transition to sound with very few problems. Also, sound did not entice them into using much verbal humor, and this quality helps to keep their films from becoming dated. Most of the Laurel and Hardy material is still consistently funny many decades after the films were produced.

Laurel and Hardy had been appearing in sound shorts for approximately two years before they made the transition to the longer feature film format. They had made an appearance in an MGM feature, *The Rogue Song,* in 1930, but their first official feature effort, *Pardon Us,* was not produced until 1931. The pace of this film is somewhat erratic, but their second feature, *Pack Up Your*

Troubles (1932), possesses much smoother and coherent movement. Used to maintaining a 20-minute format (or occasionally a 30-minute running time in the three-reel shorts), they experienced difficulty extending their material to a 60-minute, or longer, length.

By 1933, the team had begun to master the longer format, at first in *The Devil's Brother,* which blends comedy with music, and the superb *Sons of the Desert,* a film that possibly includes Laurel and Hardy's greatest combination of execution, pace, and style. The subsequent features, particularly *Our Relations* (1936), *Way Out West* (1937), and *Block-Heads* (1938), all contain well-paced narratives as well as the classic style that the team had perfected in the short film format.

Music is used sporadically in the early sound period, but by 1930, the team began to use several composers who wrote jazz numbers to use as background music in the films. Certain swing themes can be heard in a great number of the shorts and some of the features, adding a familiarity which seems to become part of the Stan and Ollie characters. At times, this music is part of the diagesis, or on-screen action, emanating from a radio or a big band at a nightclub. This style is somewhat peculiar to the comedy film, and the few shorts and features which do not include it seem interrupted when the more traditional incidental film music is used.

Diegetic music is featured in several films in which Stan and Ollie sing and dance. Oliver Hardy had been trained as a vocalist, and his fine voice can be heard in *Brats, Beau Hunks* (1931), *Pardon Us, Sons of the Desert,* and *The Flying Deuces* (1939). Stan Laurel sings (in a dubbed low bass and a high soprano, respectively) in *The Bohemian Girl* (1936), and both men sing a duet in *Below Zero* (1930), *Way Out West,* and *Swiss Miss* (1938).

Way Out West includes the team's most memorable dancing scene, in which they perform a ballet-like jig to the music of the Avalon Boys Quartet. Although this sequence is one of Laurel and Hardy's most famous, it is the last of three such scenes in their work. The first dance appears in *The Music Box,* with Stan and Ollie performing a soft-shoe on the end of a piano crate.

The second and most elaborate dancing sequence appears in one of their most unusual feature-length films, *Bonnie Scotland* (1935). Diegetic music dominates this scene, in which soldiers Stan and Ollie elegantly prance and kick to a Scottish jig played by a regimental

brass band. Lasting several minutes, the dance features the two men attempting to pick up trash, mistakenly including Sergeant Finlayson (James Finlayson) in the proceedings, and ultimately skipping themselves directly into jail. A final flourish is provided when Stan and Ollie close the cell door, toss away the key, and, bending over, wave their kilts at the sergeant.

These strange scenes are delightfully cinematic, with Laurel and Hardy providing a purely *visual* element accompanied only by synchronized music. The sequence in *Bonnie Scotland* is not only the longest, but proves to be the most effective, combining the consistently inventive pantomime of the team with the excellent cinematography of Art Lloyd and the unobtrusive editing of Bert Jordan, and, uncredited, Stan Laurel. This is merely one example of the quality of Laurel and Hardy's material in this underrated film, which has been criticized for its somewhat superfluous romantic subplot.

Sound also offered Laurel and Hardy the ability to enter an entirely new film genre, the musical. Hal Roach and the team practically invented the subgenre of the comic opera and they produced five films of this kind between 1930 and 1938. These films are peculiar in that they are basically the popular cinematic operetta of the early 1930s combined with the comedy of Stan and Ollie.

What appears to be an absurd combination is quite successful at times, and this experimentation produced one of the team's best films, *The Devil's Brother,* in 1933. Music serves an actual narrative purpose in this film, instead of merely providing background or a pleasant diversion. Fra Diavolo (Dennis King), a notorious bandit who is terrorizing the Italian countryside, sings a distinctive song to announce his arrival to others. Whenever this tune is sung, people within hearing distance realize that danger is soon to come.

In one scene, "Ollio," pretending to be the feared villain, sings the tune to the real Fra Diavolo. The pseudo-bandit realizes his predicament when Diavolo begins to sing the correct version of the song. Diavolo then orders that Ollio be hanged. A later scene involves the bandit's plan to rob the home of an aristocrat (James Finlayson). He enlists "Stanlio" and Ollio, informing them that,

Opposite: Sergeant Finlayson orders Stan and Ollie to clean up the Indian army base in *Bonnie Scotland* (1935) — a command that inspires the Boys to create one of their finest screen moments, superbly combining the visual with the musical.

when he sings a certain song, they are to aid him in burglarizing the palace. Standing on a balcony high above his "accomplices," Diavolo begins to whisper the song, but Stanlio and Ollio are unable to hear him. The frustrated criminal repeats the song, more loudly each time, taking the risk of arousing the sleeping owners.

Music also serves a narrative purpose in *Our Relations,* in which Laurel and Hardy portray Stan and Ollie and their twin brothers, Alf and Bert. Several sequences include both pairs of characters, dressed in identical clothing. In order to avoid audience confusion, a musical leitmotiv is used for each pair—the Laurel and Hardy theme ("Call of the Cuckoo," by Marvin Hatley) is played when Stan and Ollie appear, with sailors Alf and Bert being accompanied by Sir Henry Wood's famous hornpipe from "Fantasia on British Sea Songs." These scenes, involving two Laurels and two Hardys, could not have been successfully depicted in a silent film (unless a large number of cumbersome title cards were included). Without the use of this musical score, *Our Relations* would not make any sense. This aspect shows that, by 1936, Laurel and Hardy were using techniques created for the sound film, including them with the classic technique created in the silent period.

The other comic operas include *The Rogue Song,* a lost film directed by Lionel Barrymore and Hal Roach, *Babes in Toyland* (1934), a whimsical comedy/fantasy/horror film based on the Victor Herbert operetta, *The Bohemian Girl,* which includes a superb music score, adapted from the 1843 opera by Michael W. Balfe, and *Swiss Miss.*

One of the creations of the Laurel and Hardy–Hal Roach films is the use of the sound effect (something that was soon appropriated by other comics and cartoon filmmakers in the 1930s). Often-used sound effects in these films consist of a clanging or woodblock sound when someone is hit on the head or the sound of an explosion when a mechanical device malfunctions. Offscreen sounds are also used to suggest an event thought to be too terrible (or difficult) to actually show on-screen (such as the car wreck scene at the end of *Hog Wild*). The use of these sound effects adds yet another surreal dimension to Stan and Ollie's exaggerated actions.

V.

The Boys as Couple

> "We're just like two peas in a pot."
> —Stan, *Sons of the Desert* (1933)

"Really to me they were always The Boys," reminisced Leo McCarey. "By the time I got engrossed with the possibility of their being a team, they had become almost like my sons—or maybe my *brothers* would be a little more accurate. My crazy brothers from the next town over."[1]

By the time sound reached the Laurel and Hardy films, the two men were referred to as "the Boys" by characters on-screen—wives, policemen, businessmen, and assorted others. This term is a perfect way to describe the characters of Stan and Ollie, who, physiologically, are grown men, but, psychologically, are still small children.

In 1954, Oliver Hardy made a perceptive comment when he stated that "these two fellows we created, they are nice, very nice people. They never get anywhere because they are both so very dumb but they don't *know* that they're dumb. One of the reasons why people like us, I guess, is because they feel so superior to us. Even an eight-year-old kid can feel superior to us, and that makes him laugh."[2]

The Boys literally are just boys, children who attempt to act like mature human beings. A constant and frustrating paradox exists for Stan and Ollie—they are humans who inhabit grown male bodies, but they cannot actively function as men. Like the behavior of young children who try to emulate grown-ups, each instance in which either of them attempts to perform as a mature person is quickly transformed into a total disaster. At times, they begin to participate in mature activities (smoking, drinking, contact with the opposite sex, marriage), but do not possess sufficient development and experience to bring them to a successful conclusion.

35

Stan is a character who, by psychological standards, is approximately six years old. Stan has yet to attain the reality principle, a being whose "mental processes have an inexhaustible interest. Stan is like a child who is still learning by imitation and cannot grasp abstractions or make any jump in reasoning."[3]

Their First Mistake (1932), and what appears to be its companion piece, *Towed in a Hole* (1932), both directed by George Marshall, are two films which greatly elaborate the Stan character. In the former, Stan becomes a baby, and the latter features him as a slightly older child, who causes accidents while playing and is sent to his room by Ollie.

Stan's penchant for the "rhetoric strangle" is a direct result of his still developing mind. He is never fully able to understand what he or other characters are saying, unless content is made simple and explicit. He actually has no long-term memory, as he is unable to properly store linguistic terms for future use. Syllables from one word frequently become combined with those of another, and synonyms and metaphorical expressions do not exist for him.

One of Stan's most typical behaviors involves his rendering of well-known adages and literary quotes. In *Brats,* when he attempts to provide an analogy for a proper method of child care, he informs Ollie that "you can lead a horse to water, but a pencil must be lead." In *The Laurel-Hardy Murder Case* (1930), when he attempts to determine what day Christmas falls on, Stan states, "The day before Christmas — November fifteenth. . ." (counting on fingers) "Septober, October, Nowonder. . ."

A great number of the sound films feature this confusion, but *Tit for Tat* contains what is perhaps the strangest reference of all. In Act III, Scene III of Shakespeare's *Othello,* Iago states:

> Who steals my purse steals trash — 'tis something,
>   nothing
> 'Twas mine, 'tis his, and has been slave to thousands;
> But he that filches from me my good name
> Robs me of that which not enriches him
> And makes me poor indeed

In an attempt to console Ollie, who has had his reputation "maliciously trodden upon" by Mr. Hall (Charlie Hall), Stan says, "He who filters your good name, steals trash."

Possibly the Hollywood cinema's most complex "couple" — the vacuous Stanley and the disgusted Ollie.

Although Stan's references are always arcane and completely illogical, Ollie is somehow able to understand them. He usually gives an affirmative nod of the head, or replies, "You know, Stanley, I think you're right." Since Ollie is the only other person who is similar in being to Stan, he is able to comprehend what others would consider to be mere gibberish.

A further evidence of Stan's limited mental capacity lies in the area of short-term memory storage. On certain occasions, Stan will attempt to aid his companion by proposing a solution to a pressing problem. Seconds later, when Ollie asks him to repeat what he has just said, he delivers a garbled version of the previous communication. It appears that Stan has no rehearsal capability, and cannot properly store his own speech. He is able to initially formulate an idea, but once it has been transformed into a verbal message, it is lost forever.

In *Towed in a Hole,* the Boys are fish salesmen who peddle their product on the street — Ollie drives, while Stan blows a large toy horn. Just as Ollie has finished stating that their business is doing well, Stan offers the following economic suggestion:

> You know, Ollie ... I've been thinking. I know how we could make a lot more money. If we caught our own fish ... we wouldn't have to pay for it, and, whoever we sold it to ... it would be clear profit (He then blows the horn, loudly).

Ollie stops the auto in the middle of the street, asking, "Let me hear that again." With a slightly perplexed look on his face, Stan attempts to reconstruct his idea:

> Well, if you caught a fish, and whoever you sold it to ... they wouldn't have to pay for it. Then, the profits ... they would go to the fish. If you ... if you ... (He blows the horn once more).

The Fixer-Uppers, one of their last short films, includes Stan giving yet another dose of helpful advice. Acting as door-to-door Christmas card salesmen in Paris, the Boys encounter a depressed woman (Mae Busch) who is being neglected by her husband. The boys engage in the following dialogue, with Stan attempting to cheer up the woman:

STAN: You know what? I knew a woman once that had a case just like yours, but do you know what she did? She got a fellow to make love to her in front of her husband, and it made the husband jealous.

OLLIE: Then what happened?

STAN: Well ... eh?

OLLIE: So what?

STAN: Well, when the husband got jealous, his wife knew he was in love with her, just because he was jealous. So, you see, and if he hadn't have been jealous, then he wouldn't have paid any attention to the fella that made him jealous ... see?

OLLIE: Well, what did the husband do? Take a gun and go out and shoot the other fellow?

STAN: No, when the husband found out that he was so pleased that he was jealous, he took his wife in his arms, and he kissed her, and they went out again, and they got married all over. And then, he kissed her again, and...

OLLIE: Now, just a minute. What happened to the other fellow?

STAN: Well, when the husband found out he was jealous, he was so pleased that the other fella had made him jealous, he gave the other fella a lot of money, because he'd made him jealous. And, they ... they all lived happy ever after.

OLLIE: That's a splendid idea.

After Ollie is offered $50 to "make love" to the woman, he wants to make sure that he thoroughly understands Stan's story. Moving his friend off to the side of the room, he commands, "Tell me again about the fella who made love to the wife."

Stan retells the tale:

Well, when the husband found out that the other fella was jealous, he ... he took him in his arms, and then he ... he gave his wife a lot of money ... and then he kissed the other fella, because he made him jealous ... and ... they went out ... and ... then, they all lived happy ever after.

Thoroughly satisfied, Ollie pats his friend on the shoulder, having no idea that this version differed from the first. Several minutes later, the enraged husband (Charles Middleton) returns, catching Ollie and his wife in a lustful embrace.

Demanding to know the meaning of the encounter, the husband forces Stan to tell his story a third and final time: "I remember a fella once that had a jealous wife, and..."

Fortunately, Stan is spared any further confusion by the offended Parisian, who challenges Ollie to a duel to the death. By means of his rhetoric strangle, Stan not only exhibits his retarded state of development, but also places his companion in a very precarious position. *The Fixer-Uppers* is the only film in which Stan attempts to relate the same anecdote three times, comprising a large portion of an entire sequence.

The visual and verbal reaction that most identifies Stan Laurel is his cry. First used to good effect in *Get 'Em Young* (1926), the device became a staple soon after his collaboration with Hardy began. Laurel continually claimed that he disliked the technique, thinking it to be unnecessary, but it is an aspect of the Stan character that is absolutely essential. The reaction that a child most commonly issues when he or she is hurt or perplexed is a cry, attempting to alleviate stress or to gain sympathy from others, particularly older persons. No matter how angry Ollie may become, Stan's crying forces him to empathize with his partner. This device may seem maudlin on the surface, but it never ceases to constitute some of the most humorous moments in the films.

Even when performing the simplest of tasks, Stan experiences constant coordination problems and cannot adapt to the routine that most normal people follow. In *The Second One Hundred Years* (1927), he performs his calisthenic movements in reverse order, while the other prisoners perfectly follow the instructor. *Scram* (1932) includes a scene in which Ollie tries to boost Stan up to a window. When Ollie kneels down on the ground to provide a step for his partner, Stan kneels down beside him.

Coordination is always difficult for Stan if he attempts to copy another person's actions. However, he displays amazing feats of physical dexterity when he is allowed to create activity himself. In *The Devil's Brother,* Stanlio performs two distinct games of dexterity — "Earsie, Eyesie, Nosie" and "Finger-Wiggle." Throughout the narrative, he casually plays these games, driving others who cannot match his abilities slowly insane. *Babes in Toyland* also shows Stan at his dexterous best, playing a combination of baseball and golf called "Pee-Wee." In both films, Ollie is unable to perform any of Stan's creations.

In several films, Stan cannot read, write, or tell time. In *Double*

Whoopee (1929), he goes through a meticulous preparatory process with a hotel guest register, holding the book in various positions and adjusting his stance, before finally marking an "X" below Ollie's signature. In *Bacon Grabbers* (1929), he looks at his watch, which reads 5:00 P.M., stops working, and begins to eat his lunch. Sitting down to look at a newspaper in *Blotto* (1930), Stan skims through it for several moments before realizing that it is printed in Hebrew. *The Devil's Brother* features a scene in which Stan scrutinizes a document for approximately one minute and then glances at Ollie, asking, "What's it say?"

The inadequacy of Stan's brain is further illustrated in *Saps at Sea* (1940), when his neurons apparently fire in an extremely delayed manner. After he backs over Ollie and crashes through a brick wall with their Model T, Ollie hits Stan on the head with a brick. Stan idly sits in the driver's seat, with a blank look on his face. After several seconds, he starts up violently, exclaiming, "Ouch!" and rubbing his assaulted cranium.

Stan's existence as a child is further reinforced in an early scene of *Sons of the Desert*. Returning from a meeting, the Boys arrive at their adjacent apartments. When he is informed that Stan's wife has gone duck hunting, Ollie requests that his friend, who does not want to stay home alone, be allowed to spend the evening at the Hardy household. Ollie's wife reluctantly agrees, providing the meek Stan with a "babysitter."

Ollie, who exhibits characteristics slightly more developed than Stan, is a person who attempts to exist in a world free from care, much like a child who becomes upset when another child takes one of his toys. He plays big brother to Stan, continually attempting to provide helpful advice. This supervision inevitably backfires, causing an escalation of an already pertinent problem. According to Charles Barr, "Ollie will not compromise: if things are not going to be perfect, let them be wrecked thoroughly."[4]

Ollie has a desire to feel superior to Stan, constantly giving him orders and expecting them to be carried out. Quite often, however, Ollie exhibits this behavior because he is afraid to perform a duty himself, and would rather have Stan suffer the supposed consequences. When Stan fails to live up to his expectations, Ollie frequently replies, "When I want something done, I always have to do it myself." This statement usually suggests that chaos is soon to follow.

Ollie is always literate to a certain degree, but does occasionally have trouble executing simple mathematical equations and fails to have much, if any, memory. In *Leave 'Em Laughing,* he creates a triple gag by stepping on the same tack on three different occasions. Each time, after impaling his foot with it, he tosses the tack back down onto the floor. Although his actions are just as idiotic as Stan's, Ollie attempts to maintain a facade of dignity and intelligence. Telling Stan to scale a ladder in *Bacon Grabbers,* he states, "The brains had better remain on the ground."

Quite often, Ollie attempts to impress Stan with his extensive vocabulary. In *Another Fine Mess* (1930), he commands, "Let's reconnoiter," knowing that his partner will not understand. It is Ollie's pomposity and feigned intellectual capacity that make him seem the more stupid of the two—Stan cannot help his condition, but Ollie, in part, *creates* his own stupidity.

Ollie's drive for perfection causes him to act in a manner that could be termed obsessive-compulsive—he has an obsession with neatness and a compulsion to constantly attain this state. When handling any object, such as a telephone, a glass of water, or bed covers, he *must* go through a meticulous process of gesturing and grooming before he can proceed to use it in a utilitarian manner. When doused with water, Ollie responds by wiping his eyes, lightly flinging the water away with his fingers, and giving a painfully frustrated look into the camera.

Ollie has a relationship with the camera and, indirectly, with the audience, that Stan does not experience. Whenever Stan has committed some heinous act against Ollie's person, Ollie subtly gazes at the camera/audience, attempting to gain, if not understanding, at least sympathy for his plight. In some of the early films, Stan occasionally looks at the camera, but these incidents are very sporadic, never approaching the relationship that Ollie builds with it. (Some film critics would obviously object to this technique. Stan Laurel appreciated the fantasy elements in the films, and this adds to the unreal-grounded-in-the-real atmosphere which pervades their work.)

Stan and Ollie are not only a team in the traditional sense, but actively function as a couple—they live together, share expenses, and are concerned with each other's welfare. Perhaps this brotherly relationship was best described by the late Eddie Cantor: "It is their seriousness that strikes me most forcibly. They play everything as if it might be *Macbeth* or *Hamlet*. In addition, they have two very important things going for them. One is the utter frustration of Hardy, and the other is the 'one-beat-behind-every-other-person's-thinking' of Stan. He was always late, and always wrong, and underneath that frightened face, we always get the idea that he loved Ollie."[5]

The depth of the Stan and Ollie relationship is well represented in one of their finest films, *Helpmates* (1932). Ollie has thrown a wild party during his wife's absence, and, realizing the extent of the household damage, calls Stan for help. Stan arrives within seconds, and after several mishaps, manages to clean the house for Ollie. However, while Ollie drives to the train station to pick up his wife, Stan prepares a comfortable blaze in his friend's fireplace. Upon his return, a black-eyed Ollie finds Stan swinging a garden hose, attempting to douse what remains of the smoldering house. Instead of becoming angry, Ollie accepts his friend's actions as an unfortunate accident. Sobbing, Stan asks, "Is there anything else that I can do for you?"

Many of the films contain homosexual overtones, and this aspect has either attracted too much, or too little, attention over the years. The overtones certainly are there, and not completely by accident, but Stan and Ollie are far from being practicing homosexuals. The argument that, as children, Stan and Ollie are in a pre-sexual world does not hold up in the post–Freudian era, but it can be said that they have not developed sufficiently to be able to perform sexually. Stan is even more backward than Ollie, as he is unable to make gender distinctions. Ollie must always apologize when Stan, speaking to another man, answers a question by saying, "Yes, Ma'am."

When living together, Stan and Ollie always sleep in the same bed, and the goings-on usually resemble what happens when two young boys stay all night with each other — covers are stolen, one child is kicked, or is crowded, by the other, and one makes too much noise so the other cannot sleep. Even in situations where there are two twin beds, the Boys usually sleep together in the same one. Each of them is still at the age when he feels more secure if someone else is close at hand. In *Pardon Us,* after being shown to their jail cell, they both sleep in the same cramped bunk.

The Boys are a male-bonded prototype for the male-female couples of the screwball comedies of the late 1930s and 1940s. In fact, many of the screwball comedies, especially those of Howard Hawks, deliberately borrow situations, and even dialogue, from Laurel and Hardy films. Hawks' *Bringing Up Baby* (1938) is essentially a Laurel and Hardy film with an outrageous battle of the sexes included. There are no less than 16 situations in *Bringing Up Baby* that directly resemble Laurel and Hardy material. In a 1970s interview with Joseph McBride, Hawks stated that one of his three favorite directors was Leo McCarey, who directed three, supervised 15, and wrote 20 outlines for Laurel and Hardy comedies between 1928 and 1932.[6] Obviously, McCarey's work in these short films was a strong influence on the creation of this screwball classic.

Throughout the history of the Hollywood cinema, the couple has usually been the most important unit to appear in any film, whether comic or dramatic. The final embrace usually comprises the denouement of most classic Hollywood narratives, particularly musicals and domestic dramas. The Laurel and Hardy films could be called domestic comedies, since they all involve the misadventures of a team comprised of two individuals, each of whom cannot function without the other. But unlike other screen couples, Laurel and Hardy are together in over 100 films.

In 1934, Provision IX of the newly instituted Production Code, entitled "Locations," stated: "The treatment of bedrooms must be governed by good taste and delicacy."[7] An entailment of this provision was the prohibition of showing a male-female couple in the same bed together, even if that couple was married. Twin beds, placed several feet apart, were always used in scenes such as these. In the Laurel and Hardy films, if two twin beds are shown, the Boys always get into the same one together. Stan and Ollie are not homosexuals, but it can be said that their relationship represents an alternative lifestyle.

Leo McCarey once said that he had introduced the first overtone of homosexuality, in *Putting Pants on Philip,* when Ollie attempts to tear Philip's kilt off in order to replace it with a pair of trousers. McCarey revived this material in *Liberty,* in the scene in which Stan and Ollie try to exchange clothes at various times, with policemen and other bystanders looking on. One incident features a man and a woman (Jean Harlow), opening a car door to find the Boys in the back seat, tugging at each other's trousers.

Their First Mistake is possibly their most complex film, with

Stan and Ollie performing various roles at different stages of the film — those of baby, mother, and father. Near the beginning of the narrative, after Ollie has had an argument with his wife, the two run into Stan's apartment and lie down on the bed. When Stan begins discussing their plans for "going out tonight," Ollie emphatically states that his wife won't let him go. "She thinks I think more of you than I do of her," he tells Stan.

Pondering the statement for a moment, Stan asks, "Well, you do, don't you?"

Ollie replies by mumbling, "Well, we won't go into that."

In order to console Ollie, Stan develops an idea that, if his partner should adopt a baby, it would keep his wife occupied and "all his troubles would be over." The following scene depicts Stan and Ollie returning with a baby. When Ollie summons his wife, in order to tell her the good news, he discovers that she is no longer at home. Soon, a writ server (Billy Gilbert) enters, informing Ollie that he is being sued for divorce. Turning to Stan, he forcefully tells the sad-faced homebreaker that he is being sued for "the alienation of Mr. Hardy's affection." Surveying Stan from head to toe, the writ server adds, "She'll take you hook, line, and sinker." Sighing, Stan attempts to leave, but Ollie refuses to let him go.

"You're the one who wanted me to *have* a baby," he emotes to Stan, "and now that you've got me into this trouble, you want to walk out and leave me flat."

"I don't know anything about babies," Stan meekly replies, "I have my future, my career to think of."

Incredibly flustered, Ollie responds with, "What about me? What will my friends say? Why, I'll be ostracized."

In a later scene, the two attempt to feed the baby. While Ollie tries to quiet the child, Stan begins to unbutton his nightshirt, glancing down at his chest. Here, several close-ups of Ollie are used, each showing him in a state of complete disbelief. The scene cuts back to Stan, who pulls a baby bottle from his shirt. "I put it there to keep it warm," he mutters.

The climactic scene of *Their First Mistake* is the most outrageous image to appear in any of the films. Stan, Ollie, and the baby are all sleeping in the same bed, with Stan in the middle. When the baby begins to cry, Ollie, still half asleep, pulls a bottle from a night stand. Reaching across the bed, he first places the nipple into Stan's eye and then into his mouth. As Stan sucks the milk from the bottle, the baby ceases to cry. Ollie grabs a second bottle, again sticking it into his friend's mouth, causing Stan to suck so voraciously that he swallows the nipple. Ollie then awakens, telling Stan that he should be ashamed of himself. This scene overtly stresses the role of Stan as a young child, actually showing him acting like a baby in a close-up.

Stan also acts like an infant in *Pack Up Your Troubles,* in which he climbs into a little girl's baby bed in order to hide from the authorities. When the police and a social worker arrive to retrieve the child that Stan and Ollie have "kidnapped," Stan sits in the bed, smiling, innocently holding the little girl's rag doll. In an earlier scene, Stan sits in a rocking chair, while the child lulls him to sleep by telling him the story of "The Three Bears." This bizarre incident prompts a tit for tat between the Boys, culminating with Ollie hitting Stan over the head with a baseball bat. Much like their behavior in *Their First Mistake* (which was released immediately after *Pack Up Your Troubles*), the Boys act like small children *and* like parents who are caring for a small child.

Towed in a Hole, based on an outline written by Stan Laurel, is, in many ways, a sequel to *Their First Mistake,* and may be the finest of all the sound shorts. In this film, Stan and Ollie are fish salesmen who decide to buy their own boat in order to cut out the middleman. The bulk of the narrative consists of the Boys attempting to renovate a wreck that they purchase at a nearby junkyard. Soon after work begins, Stan causes several accidents, which prompts Ollie to send him to his room in the cabin below.

While sitting alone, Stan seeks alleviation from boredom. In one long take, Stan entertains himself by doing a finger-wiggle game, fiddling with his hat, and playing tick-tack-toe with himself. Soon after "winning" the game, he draws a chalk figure of Ollie on the wall of the cabin. Observing the drawing, and then looking out the window at Ollie, Stan pokes the figure in the eye.

Charles Barr comments that

> the infant who hasn't yet mastered the reality principle is surrounded by a world which is still alive for him, a world with "magic" potential.

Given faith, why shouldn't the world of objects and cause-and-effect be willed into obeying the ego? Stan tries sympathetic magic in *Towed in a Hole:* shut away by Ollie to keep him from mischief, he draws a face on the wall, labels 'it "Ollie," and pokes it in the eye.[8]

This phenomenon, which Laurel referred to as "white magic," is also practiced by Stan in other films. He uses his thumb as a cigarette lighter in *Way Out West,* his entire hand as a tobacco pipe in *Block-Heads* (1938), and wiggles his ears frantically in *Blotto* (1930), *Any Old Port,* and *A Chump at Oxford* (1940).

The final scene of *Towed in a Hole* has Ollie freeing Stan, who has been bound to a barrel (in a previous off-camera moment). Ollie leads Stan by the hand, opens the door to the Model T, and helps him inside. This gesture draws the events of *Their First Mistake* and *Towed in a Hole* into a complete whole. Stan has become Ollie's baby in the former, and Ollie assumes the responsibility of being his father in the latter. This overt stressing of their relationship strengthens the suggestion of a familial bond between the two that pervades the other films.

Like some other couples, Stan and Ollie's lives are filled with senseless arguments and violence. Conflict inevitably arises between the two, usually because of Ollie's plans or attempts to force Stan to do the lion's share of the work. When Ollie pushes, Stan protests, and confrontation occurs. Ollie's sarcastic "Why don't you do something to help me?" is heard in many of the films, predominantly uttered when he is unable to perform a task by himself. Ollie always discovers, much too late, that it was a mistake to ask for assistance.

The Flying Deuces contains many interesting moments, one of which determines the movement of the entire film. After Ollie proposes to a young French woman (Jean Parker), she declines his offer, sending him into the depths of depression. Making a direct reference to his relationship with Stan, he sadly comments, "Just when I wanted something real ... something *wholesome.*"

Ollie decides to kill himself, and wants Stan to go with him. When Stan refuses, Ollie informs him that "people will stare at you and wonder what you are, and I won't be there to tell them." After a Foreign Legion officer convinces Ollie not to commit suicide, Stan lists the reasons why he should live: "There's your dog and there's me."

An early scene in *Way Out West* includes one of the most

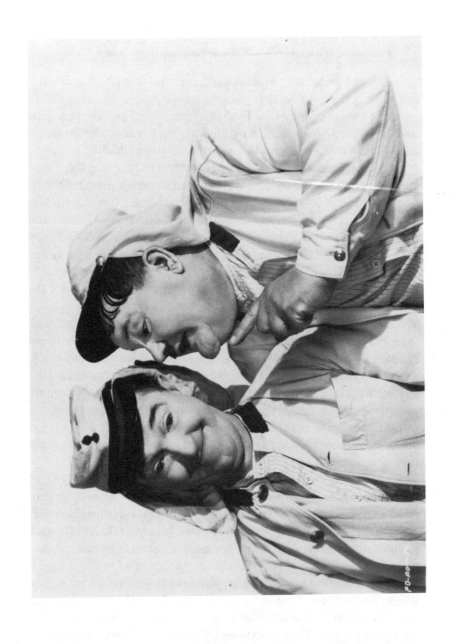

humorous and visually bizarre incidents ever performed by Laurel and Hardy. A parody of a famous moment in Frank Capra's *It Happened One Night* (1934), the sequence features Stan attempting to hitch a ride for Ollie and himself. As he stands at the side of the road, he thumbs furiously, but no stagecoach will stop to pick them up. As one coach speeds by, Stan pulls up his right pants leg, thrusting his bared calf (à la Claudette Colbert) out at the two male drivers. The sound of skidding tires is heard on the soundtrack, as the stagecoach quickly comes to a halt. The Boys, overjoyed, then run toward the conveyance, tie their pack mule to the wagon frame, and jump in.

An amusing variation on their established relationship occurs in the superlative *Our Relations*. Including Laurel and Hardy as the Boys and their twins, Alf and Bert, the film contains references to Shakespeare's *A Comedy of Errors*. Thought to have been hanged at sea, Alf and Bert obtain shore leave at the city in which their brothers reside, causing numerous cases of mistaken identity that threaten Stan and Ollie's relationships with their wives, policemen, and a local politician. The most interesting aspect of *Our Relations* is the presence of the twins, who act *exactly* like their identical brothers in every respect, presenting another pair of human beings who are just as bizarre and backward as Stan and Ollie.

In this film, Stan and Ollie engage in a ritual behavior that is a combination of a children's game and strange literary references. At several points in the narrative, both characters utter the same dialogue simultaneously. Each time this occurs, Stan, touching Ollie's nose with his index finger, states, "Shakespeare." Ollie replies by stating, "Longfellow," as he touches Stan's nose. After this practice is completed, a question is asked by one of them, and, after an answer is provided, both may return to their previous activity. Although they both have wives in *Our Relations,* the Boys spend all their available time together, creating the most intimate version of their cinematic relationship. Appearing in this film, Laurel and Hardy give what are possibly their finest performances, with their sense of timing reaching an almost supernatural level.

The ultimate experience in the Stan and Ollie relationship occurs

Opposite: Stan and his partner join the Foreign Legion in an effort to help Ollie forget about his sweetheart in *The Flying Deuces* (1939).

in the final scene of their last short film, *Thicker Than Water* (1935), also based on an outline written by Stan Laurel. Ollie, who has been knocked unconscious by his wife, is rushed to the hospital by Stan. Later, when Stan goes to visit his companion, a doctor informs him that Ollie, who needs a transfusion in order to live, has suggested that "his closest friend" provide the blood. Stan initially complains that he will have to remove his hat, but agrees to participate in the procedure.

During the operation, too much of Stan's blood goes into Ollie's body, so the doctor orders the nurse to "take some of Mr. Hardy's blood and give it to Mr. Laurel." Following the doctor's orders, the nurse begins this procedure, but the transfusion apparatus explodes. The scene then dissolves to the Boys, walking out of the operating room. In a beautifully acted sequence, Stan has taken on the physical appearance and voice of Ollie and his partner now possesses Stan's physical and vocal attributes. By experiencing this transformation, Stan and Ollie have achieved the ultimate coupling by actually becoming each other.

VI.
The Boys and Physical Objects

"Did you fellows carry that piano
all the way up these stairs?"
—postman, *The Music Box* (1932)

The Stan and Ollie coupling is well represented in their relation-ship to physical objects. Even the most commonplace device appears to acquire a life of its own when the Boys are involved, usually serv-ing one of two functions—either fulfilling a psychological need or creating an insurmountable obstacle.

The Boys' inability to function as mature human beings is reflected in their fetishistic attachment to their bowler hats. Both of them *must* be wearing this symbol of class in order to perform even the simplest of actions. Stan seems more concerned about it than does Ollie, but complete confusion overtakes both of them if the hats ever get exchanged. The first film depicting the team in the famous headgear, *Do Detectives Think?*, includes a scene in which Stan and Ollie get the hats mixed up, with Stan donning Ollie's hat and vice versa. This is the gag most repeated in the films, reaching its zenith in a triple-gag in *The Music Box.*

Almost as important as the bowler hat is the Ford Model T. The Boys' inability to exist within a world of adults is symbolized by the way in which they operate an automobile. Not only do Stan and Ollie inhibit their own progress, but they also prevent others from ac-complishing even the most routine goals. In *Leave 'Em Laughing,* they cause a citywide traffic jam when they stop to laugh at a policeman. *Two Tars* shows them complicating an already existing traffic jam and starting a domino effect of destruction that comprises most of the narrative.

Scores of Model Ts are destroyed throughout their work, the first being in *Leave 'Em Laughing,* when it sinks into a muddy hole.

Various fates await the Model T, including explosions, dismantlings, crushings, and immersions. Stan and Ollie directly cause the demolition of their auto in *One Good Turn* (1931), when, as they are fighting, it completely falls apart. In many films, the Model T is their only possession, and, when it is destroyed, they usually become completely helpless.

The most outrageous encounter between the Boys and an auto occurs in *Our Wife* (1931). To aid his friend in an elopement, Stan rents a car and drives it to the home of Ollie's fiancée. After managing to get his sweetheart out of a second-story window, Ollie proceeds toward the vehicle, only to realize that Stan has rented an Austin midget coupe. Having no time to spare, the frustrated groom settles for less, first helping the overweight woman into the front seat, and then shoving his own fat frame in. Stan then crawls in and attempts to climb over the two people and into the back. In the process, he loses his hat (which he attempts to retrieve), kicks Ollie in the head, and smashes his own face against the windshield several times. He eventually manages to get into the backseat, and all seems well, until the three realize that their suitcase is still sitting on the sidewalk outside. Ollie painfully pulls the grip into the remaining space, the car starts with a whiplash effect, and Stan's head pops up through the roof.

Aside from being hilarious and indescribably bizarre, this content perfectly illustrates one of the major Laurel and Hardy paradigms: human beings have to constantly adapt to a less-than-ideal environment in order to survive. A similar sequence, involving a phone booth, appears in *Our Relations.*

Other mechanical and electrical devices equally perplex Stan and Ollie. Stan cannot operate even simple tools, and always creates chaos when he does. His inability to use a saw in *The Finishing Touch* and *Towed in a Hole* results in Ollie falling many feet to the hard ground. In *Busy Bodies* (1933), he shears off part of his partner's trousers while planing a board and then attempts to replace the cloth by gluing it to Ollie's underwear.

Musical instruments present a myriad of problems for them in *You're Darn Tootin',* in which they disrupt an entire orchestra, and *Below Zero,* when, as street musicians, they incite a bystander into bashing Ollie over the head with a bass viol and tossing Stan's harmonium into the snow-covered street, where it is run over by a truck.

Horns drive Ollie to a nervous breakdown in *Saps at Sea,* the film ending with the Boys going to jail because of Stan's trombone playing.

The piano is the musical instrument most frequently used by Stan and Ollie, and it receives much the same treatment as does the Model T. An object of artistry and potential beauty, the destruction of a piano may signify the apathetic and oblivious attitude many people have toward art. Stan and Ollie cause a piano to be damaged in *Wrong Again,* when they place a horse on top of it, and in *Big Business,* Stan chops an upright to pieces with an axe. An early moment in *Beau Hunks* features Ollie flying into the air and landing on top of his piano, crushing it to bits, and a delivery boy, caught up in the violence of the Boys, smashes Ollie's piano in *Me and My Pal* (1933).

Pianos give away their hiding places in *Night Owls* (1930), in which they stuff a bear rug under the lid, while Stan jumps on the top, and in *Way Out West,* while hiding inside the piano, they are forced out through the bottom by enraged saloon owner Mickey Finn (James Finlayson).

The most apocalyptic use of a piano comes in *The Music Box,* their Academy Award–winning short. Hired by a wealthy woman to deliver her husband's birthday present, the Boys attempt to carry the crated instrument up an enormous flight of stairs. In this film, the piano is the major obstacle, the conflict existing between Stan and Ollie and the instrument. After four trips (three walking and one riding), they finally manage to get the leviathan inside the house. When the husband, a professor, arrives, he becomes enraged, chopping the piano apart with an axe. Ollie merely smiles, asking the angry man to sign the invoice. A similar incident appears in *Swiss Miss,* in which Stan and Ollie try to transport a piano across a footbridge in the Swiss Alps, with the typical result.

A simple home doorbell is the device that gives Stan and Ollie, and others, the most trouble. An omen of imposing danger, the ring of a doorbell signals to the apartment dweller or homeowner that the Boys have arrived. Ollie usually insists, with characteristic pomposity, that he, not Stan, ring the doorbell, typically resulting in the outside cord being torn from the front door and the inside bell being flung from the wall, flying out a window, and hitting Ollie, or someone else, on the head. The doorbell ring is a comic warning for further destruction to come.

Ollie's nemesis, water (or another similar liquid), is used in liberal quantities in almost every short and feature. Wherever Ollie may be, he continually manages, by himself, or with his friend's help, to become thoroughly soaked with water. Usually the wetness comes from the end result of a fall, sinking into an inconspicuous hole, or a garden hose, but it is often initiated by Stan. This incident is always humiliating to Ollie, especially when he is attempting to complete some serious work. The danger occurs whenever he asks his partner to aid him in his task, as in *Hog Wild,* when Stan, carrying an antenna wire across the roof of Ollie's home, causes Ollie to trip, slide down the roof, and fall into a lily pond.

Another liquid causes almost as many problems as does water: alcohol. Like small children who try liquor to "see what it is like," Stan and Ollie do not need much in order to become intoxicated and to begin committing irrational acts. Drunks have consistently been a prop for comedians, but the Laurel and Hardy version is just as bizarre as many of the other aspects of their comedy.

Blotto contains the first Stan and Ollie booze scenes, and, in this case, intoxication is caused by a placebo. Stan, wanting to go out for a night on the town with Ollie, asks his wife, who characteristically refuses. Following Ollie's plan, Stan forges a telegram which states that he must go away on important business. His wife discovers the ruse and, in order to exact her revenge, gets the "bottle she's been saving since Prohibition," pours the contents down the kitchen sink, and replaces the liquor with a mixture of iced tea, tabasco sauce, and various spices.

Obtaining a table at the Rainbow Club, Stan and Ollie attempt to secretly imbibe the "liquor." After taking one drink, Ollie makes a painful facial expression, stating, "You certainly can tell good liquor when you taste it." Agreeing, Stan quaffs an entire glass within seconds, causing his ears to wiggle at an incredible rate. After two glasses, both of them begin to laugh hysterically (a gag used frequently in their work), until Stan's wife arrives with a shotgun and chases them out of the club.

The Boys directly oppose the United States government in *Pardon Us,* when they are jailed for brewing bootleg beer. When they decide to brew 15 gallons, Ollie tells Stan, "What we don't drink, we'll sell."

Scram presents an interesting variation on the booze scenes in

Blotto. Invited home by a drunk (Arthur Housman), Stan and Ollie enjoy silk robes, cigars, and not knowing they are in the wrong place, a conversation with the woman of the house (Vivien Oakland). Fainting when she sees two strange men in her husband's pajamas, the wife is revived by Ollie, who gives her a glass of water, which is actually bootleg liquor left by the drunk. Soon, the wife is laughing hysterically, causing Stan and Ollie to repeat their routine from *Blotto.* The Boys have a similar experience in *Them Thar Hills* (1934), in which they get a traveler's wife (Mae Busch) intoxicated, again not knowing that their "water" is liquor.

Three films highlight Stan as a dysfunctioning drunk — *The Devil's Brother, The Bohemian Girl,* and *Swiss Miss.* In the first two, Ollie is ultimately responsible for Stan's consumption of large quantities of wine.

The closing scenes of *The Devil's Brother* feature the Boys in the wine cellar of an aristocrat, gathering wine for a wedding feast. As Ollie stands on a ladder, filling steins with the liquor, Stan waits below him, pouring the wine into a large container. When the container becomes full, Stan can only think of one other place to put the wine that Ollie is still handing to him — his stomach. After he has drunk several pints of booze, Ollie remarks that his friend is "spiffed," as they prepare to transport the wine up to the reception. Another laughing scene follows, with Stan getting up to stumble into the party. A sword duel between two characters commences, with Stan foiling the villain by running in front of his sword with a barrel of liquor.

A similar incident occurs in *The Bohemian Girl,* when Ollie enlists Stan to bottle homemade wine. Ollie leaves for his "zither lesson," allowing Stan to remain and finish his work. What follows is some of the best comedy in all of the Laurel and Hardy films, with Stan attempting to get the wine into the bottles. Unable to stop the flow through the siphon, Stan puts it into his mouth between fillings. He proceeds to fill several containers in this manner, using a slightly different technique each time. Eventually, he runs out of bottles and drinks the barrel dry. Ollie returns, suggesting that he and Stan rescue their female friend, who has been captured by oppressive rulers. During the rescue, Ollie is completely ineffectual, but Stan, emboldened by the liquor, grabs a whip and, in a frenzied state, holds the evil oppressors at bay. In both of these films, it is suggested that alcohol is the only thing that can help Stan function as an effective human being.

Swiss Miss contains a variation on the material in *The Devil's Brother* and *The Bohemian Girl*. Stan and Ollie, unable to pay their bill at a Swiss hotel, are forced to work for the house chef. Assigned to chicken plucking, they sit outdoors, behind the hotel. As Stan works, he eyes a Saint Bernard that is lying nearby. The bored kitchen worker seems to be interested in the barrel of brandy that the dog has strapped around its neck, and asks Ollie what the liquor is used for. Ollie replies that "the brandy is put there for a humane purpose, and anyone who would stoop so low as to take it should be shot."

Soon, Ollie is called into the kitchen, leaving Stan alone with the dog. Thoroughly investigating the situation, he attempts to lure the animal over to him so the barrel may be removed. After several fruitless efforts, Stan develops a brilliant idea—he lies down on the ground and begins to toss chicken feathers into the air, yelling, "Help! Help! I'm freezing to death!" The Saint Bernard shuffles over to Stan, laying its head on his chest. Stan quickly removes the barrel and gulps down the brandy in seconds. A short time later, he is stumbling around, attempting to help Ollie carry a piano up into the Alps. This scene, featuring a pantomimic tour de force by Stan Laurel, strongly emphasizes the role that liquor plays in their work.

These scenes involving Stan's drunkenness all take place in European settings (Italy, Bohemia, and Switzerland), possibly suggesting that this part of the world features an atmosphere more conducive to drinking. Prohibition was still in effect when *The Devil's Brother* was released and the 1934 Production Code stated that "the use of liquor in American life, when not required by the plot or for proper characterization, will not be shown."[1] Perhaps filmmakers of the period assumed, or were persuaded, that a faraway, "liquor-filled" Europe was more probable than the depiction of such scenes in the United States.

Food also gets a fair amount of attention in their films and, many times, it is very difficult to obtain. Although Ollie is "the fat one," Stan is usually more interested in eating. In *The Second One Hundred Years,* as soon as he hears that dinner is served, Stan races to the table in front of everyone else. In various films, Ollie brings

Stan home for supper, because he has pleaded, "I want to get something to eat." Obviously, Ollie also enjoys food, as in *The Flying Deuces,* when, as a new Foreign Legion recruit, he walks up to a captain, asking, "When are we going to have dinner?"

Total chaos is created in *Come Clean* (1931), when Stan expresses a desire to eat some ice cream. After requesting "mustachio" ice cream at a nearby soda fountain, Stan manages to obtain chocolate. On their way back to Ollie's apartment, the Boys prevent a woman (Mae Busch) from committing suicide. Demanding that they take care of her, the woman proceeds to cause never-ending problems for Stan, Ollie, and their wives.

Stan's robust appetite is best represented in *The Bohemian Girl,* in which he consumes an entire breakfast for two. Seconds after Arlene (Jacqueline Wells), Ollie's foster daughter, serves breakfast to the Boys, she begins relating her previous night's dream in the form of a romantic song. Focusing his attention upon the young woman's performance, Ollie ignores his portion of the breakfast. Arlene's singing continues for several minutes, allowing Stan ample time to eat everything on the table. Following the final note of the song, Ollie glances down at the table and then up at his companion. "Of all the selfish things," Ollie forcefully states. "Why did you do it?"

"I didn't want it to go cold," Stan replies. "I didn't know how long she was going to dream." Assuming that no more breakfast exists, Ollie disgustedly begins to clear the table and wash the dirty dishes.

One of Stan's strangest obsessions involves nuts. In the team's first sound film, *Unaccustomed As We Are* (1929), Ollie invites Stan home for dinner. As the pompous host tells the anxious guest of the succulent steak meal they are about to enjoy, Stan interrupts, asking, "Any nuts?" This reference to nuts is the first recorded dialogue to be issued by Stan Laurel. Ollie's wife (Mae Busch) refuses to cook supper for Stan and walks out the door, telling Ollie that she "is never coming back." Later in the film, she returns, attempting to reconcile with Ollie by giving a large bag of nuts to Stan.

Stan repeats his "Any nuts?" query in *Pardon Us,* in which the Boys attempt to go on a hunger strike. Their appetites begin to get the best of them as a prison guard (Stanley Sandford) describes a sumptuous meal that is supposedly being served in the mess hall.

After being told that roast turkey and strawberry shortcake are included on the menu, the Boys' mouths begin to water, with Stan asking about his favorite food. "Of course, all you can eat of them," replies the guard, leading them into a dinner of cold gruel.

County Hospital (1932) involves Stan's visit to an ailing Ollie, who is laid up in the hospital with a broken leg. Stan, stating that "I had nothing else to do, so I thought I'd come around and visit you," hands Ollie a get-well gift—a bag of hard-boiled eggs and nuts. Becoming angry, Ollie tells him that he cannot eat such food, asking, "Why didn't you bring me a box of candy?"

Stan replies, "They cost too much . . . besides, you haven't paid me for the last two boxes I brought you."

Having been turned down by his friend, Stan decides to eat the gift himself. Glancing around for a nutcracker, Stan spies a large iron object, just perfect for cracking walnuts, lying on the floor beside the bed. He picks it up, begins to crack the nut, and sends Ollie's broken leg slamming into the railing at the foot of the bed. The doctor (Billy Gilbert) runs in, grabs the traction weight from Stan, and promptly flies out the window. Soon, the room is nearly destroyed and Ollie is evicted from the hospital.

The fourth major "nut" film, Oliver the Eighth (1934), features Ollie's involvement with an insane high society widow (Mae Busch). Ollie moves out, leaving Stan to operate "The Laurel and Hardy Tonsorial Parlor" on his own. After Ollie has moved in with the widow, Stan arrives, demanding that he be allowed to stay with Ollie. When his partner inquires as to what became of the barber shop, Stan replies, "I sold it . . . I mean, I swapped it."

Ollie asks, "What did you get?"

Holding up a wrapped package, Stan extracts a painted brick, proudly stating, "Look, solid gold." Rummaging into his pocket, he adds, "And look what he threw in for good measure . . . some nuts!"

The Flying Deuces also includes a scene which involves this particular type of food. When Stan tells Ollie's prospective fiancée that his friend is "nuts" about her, she hands Stan a large basket of assorted nuts.

Second only to his passion for nuts is Stan's frequent consumption of bananas (an aspect of esoterica that psychoanalytic theorists would probably enjoy discussing). When he eats a banana in The

Bohemian Girl, Ollie asks him for part of it. Extracting the last portion of fruit, Stan hands his friend the peel. *Saps at Sea* features a lengthy banana scene, in which Stan peels it, only to find several more layers of peel underneath, with no fruit to be found at the center. When he tosses the banana peels away, viewers could expect that an upcoming gag is being telegraphed. However, these actions usually create anticipation with no payoff — few people ever slip on them. In all of their work, only three scenes involve banana peel accidents (a gag usually associated with slapstick comedy) — *The Battle of the Century* (caused by Ollie), *From Soup to Nuts* (placed directly in Ollie's path by a dog), and *A Chump at Oxford* (1940), in which Stan's discarded peel aids in the capture of a bank robber.

Not only does Stan have an irrational desire for nuts and bananas, but he usually attempts to consume just about anything he can get his hands on, whether it is an edible substance or not. In *Sons of the Desert,* while waiting for Ollie to finish an argument with his wife, Stan inconspicuously grabs an apple from a nearby fruit bowl. Biting into it, he chews for minutes, making painful swallowing gestures, until Ollie informs him that "it's made of wax!" *Way Out West* features Stan, after losing a bet to Ollie, sprinkling salt on and eating his bowler hat. After a few bites, he begins to enjoy it, until Ollie grabs it away from him. Behind Stan's back, Ollie tries a bite himself, only to spit it out in disgust.

An entire synthetic meal is concocted in *Saps at Sea,* when the Boys attempt to prepare supper for an escaped convict who has shanghaied their boat. Making spaghetti and meatballs out of string, an old sponge, and red paint, bacon from a dirty kerosene wick, biscuits from talcum, and coffee from a sack of tobacco, Stan and Ollie attempt to serve the criminal what Stan refers to as a "sympathetic" meal. Becoming aware of what the Boys have done, the convict forces them to eat the meal. In an extremely painful, but hilarious, scene, Laurel and Hardy's penchant for eating the inedible is carried to extremes.

VII.
The Boys and Animals

"Poor little Laughing Gravy."
—Stan, *Laughing Gravy* (1931)

Throughout history, animals have played a major role in the legends, mythology, and religious dogma of many civilizations. The ancient Egyptians, as well as the Greeks, held certain animals in high regard, considering many to have eternal significance, simply because of their non-human *otherness*.

The Egyptians considered animals, the "non-human," to be *superhuman*. The Bible includes several references to plagues of insects, and recent civilizations have also emphasized this idea (the central European legends of vampire and werewolf). American literature of the mid-1800s featured the macabre warnings of Edgar Allan Poe, who had a special fetish for black cats and birds.

Animals have always been present in motion pictures, usually in a realistic manner—such as the horse and livestock in the western or the dog in the domestic film. The suggestion of animals having anthropomorphic or supernatural attributes has long been part of the horror film (the cat, the wolf) and, most notably, the comedy.

The animal as both foil and helpmate (particularly the dog) was used by many comic filmmakers, including Sennett and Chaplin, whose *A Dog's Life* (1918) is possibly the finest example. Animals in the Laurel and Hardy films possess an almost supernatural significance, and present a constant paradox for Stan and Ollie—both men share an affection and respect for them, but these creatures inevitably manage to create unpleasantness for the Boys.

With regard to the insect world, Stan occasionally makes strange remarks about houseflies. Although presented in a very subtle manner, the appearance, or even mere suggestion, of flies in the Laurel and Hardy films appears to foreshadow the unavoidable chaos that follows.

Chickens Come Home (1931) includes a scene in which Stan, chasing after one of the pests (heard in an incredible buzzing sound effect), slaps mayoral candidate Ollie's posh office chair with a huge flyswatter. Moments later, Ollie is in the midst of slander and blackmail in the person of an old flame (Mae Busch).

An even more unpleasant insect encounter appears in *Our Wife,* when Stan observes Ollie's wedding cake being attacked by a small swarm of flies. Alleviating the problem, Stan fills an atomizer with "Flit," a powerful insecticide, and sprays a liberal amount of the chemical mixture onto the cake. A short time later, Ollie, wishing to gargle, sprays the content of the atomizer into his mouth, causing a serious internal "fire."

"The flies won't bother us," says Stan in *Them Thar Hills,* suggesting that he and his companion rent a travel trailer in order to escape the unpleasant pests. Within hours after reaching their campsite, the conveyance is smashed to pieces.

In *A Chump at Oxford,* after being shown to their dormitory rooms, Stan claims, "No wonder people go to school . . . nice place to live in like this . . . no flies or nothin'." Soon, the dean of Oxford walks in to discover that considerable damage has been done to *his* private quarters.

A variation on the fly motif, a huge swarm of bees is featured in the final sequence of one of the team's earliest films, *With Love and Hisses* (1927). Stan plays a meek army recruit who is assigned by Sergeant Ollie to guard a pile of soldiers' uniforms as the troops swim in a nearby lake. Moments after Ollie tosses his lit cigarette into the clothing, Stan decides to join the rest of the group. Following the destruction of their uniforms, Ollie and his troops must hide themselves behind a billboard advertising the Cecil B. DeMille film *The Volga Boatman.* As the men replace the painted heads of the Russians with their own, a skunk forces them to flee, carrying the huge billboard with them. On the way back to the base, the nude men stumble over two beehives. Soon, the air is literally saturated with bees, stinging Ollie's group and all of the soldiers and top brass at the army encampment.

This gag is repeated, with slight variations, in the final scene of *Bonnie Scotland.* In order to protect themselves from a horde of attacking Indian natives, the Boys toss dozens of buzzing beehives at the unsuspecting enemy, causing an uncontrollable frenzy. After the Indians are staved off, Stan and Ollie fall into hives themselves, ultimately carrying the insect plague to their own regiment. Hundreds of British soldiers convulse, scream, and turn flips as the scene fades to black. In this film, the Boys see the use of insects as a solution to a problem, not realizing that their actions will create even worse circumstances.

The animal that appears most often with Stan and Ollie is the dog, usually a small but persistent mutt that attacks them or causes them to be evicted from their lodgings. Throughout the films, typical domestic dogs turn ferocious, chasing the Boys and revealing their cover as they attempt to hide or escape from certain unsavory characters. *Sugar Daddies* (1927) includes a scene in which Stan, as the lawyer, and his client (James Finlayson) attempt to escape from unwanted guests by disguising themselves as a very tall woman. As they make their way through a hotel lobby, a curious terrier chases them, causing Ollie, the butler, to attempt a defense.

A less antagonistic canine, Buster, appears in *Early to Bed* (1928), one of the first films to explore the complex Stan and Ollie relationship. The film opens with the Boys as vagrants, lounging on a lonely park bench. As Ollie opens his mail, he hands the refuse to Stan, who then forwards it to Buster for proper dumping into a nearby trash can. After Ollie realizes that he has inherited a fortune and the luxurious "Hardy Manor," he makes Stan his butler and Buster is given a posh bed at the estate. One evening when Ollie arrives home in a drunken state, the dog knocks him to the ground, revealing his condition to Stan, who suggests that Ollie go straight to bed. After several humiliations from his inebriated "boss," Stan threatens to quit his position as butler. When Ollie refuses to let him leave, the enraged Stan begins to destroy the furnishings of Hardy Manor, causing a tit-for-tat battle between the two men. In the midst of combat, Buster rushes in, observes the insane antics of his human companions, and quickly exits the room, never to be seen again. In this film, it appears that a dog is even intelligent enough to realize that living with the Boys is a hazardous affair.

Stan and Ollie appear as agents who attempt to repossess the delinquent Edgar Kennedy's radio in *Bacon Grabbers*. Formulating a "brilliant" idea, Ollie borrows a child's Great Dane, a ferocious animal who eats nothing but raw meat. As the determined agent approaches Kennedy's front door, the homeowner steps out, tethering an absurd mechanical canine at the end of a leash. Frightened out of its wits, the Great Dane drags Ollie down a long sidewalk and into the street, where he is almost flattened by a speeding auto.

Laughing Gravy (named after the dog that appears in the film) features Stan, Ollie, and their pet, all attempting to live together in a cramped apartment. Stan's hiccoughs continually cause the dog to bark, waking the landlord (Charlie Hall), who commands that the dog must be thrown out of the building. In a valiant effort to save their pet, the Boys become soaked with water, frozen in the snow, and covered with fireplace soot. An earlier version of this film, *Angora Love* (1929), features the same basic plot, with Stan and Ollie housing a goat instead of a dog.

This story was reworked once more in 1932 for *The Chimp,* a three-reel short that features distinct overtones of bestiality. When "Colonel Finn's Big Show," a circus revue, closes down, the Boys receive part of the show as payment for their services. Stan acquires a flea circus, while Ollie has the distinction of receiving "Ethel, the Human Chimpanzee" (actually a gorilla, played by Charles Gamora).

Billy Gilbert portrays Joe, landlord and very jealous husband, who suspects his wife of foul play. While attempting to get their gorilla to bed, Ollie yells, "Stop it Ethel, and come to bed!" Eavesdropping, Joe believes that the Boys are having an illicit affair with his wife, Ethel, who has been absent all day. Grabbing a pistol and bursting into their room, he walks over to the bed, where the gorilla has covered itself up. In an emotional frenzy, the landlord pleads, "You deceitful trifler you ... you, the bearer of my name ... the mother of my children. You know that I've loved you ... loved you more than life itself." Just as the gorilla pokes its head from beneath the blanket, Joe's wife walks into the room. Joe becomes violent, ordering the animal out, as Ollie concernedly states, "But you said you loved her."

An early scene of *The Chimp* features the two men and the gorilla being followed by a lion that has escaped from the circus. Referring to the beast as "MGM," Stan warns Ollie of the danger soon to come. Another variation on the fly motif, the flea circus also wreaks havoc on the Boys' persons when Stan drops it into their bed.

A gorilla also creates an extremely dangerous situation for Stan and Ollie in *Swiss Miss,* as the Boys attempt to carry a composer's piano across a rotting footbridge in the Swiss Alps. This bizarre sequence has prompted much discussion from Laurel and Hardy critics over the years, who have claimed that the scene, as it appears in the final release print, does not make sense. As originally scripted by Laurel, the piano was to have housed a bomb, planted there by the Boys' employer, a homicidal hotel chef, who had wired the device to a single key on the keyboard. During their trek across the mountain chasm, the intoxicated Stan was to have fallen against the keys, setting off the explosion.

As the scene stands, the gorilla, not the bomb, causes the bridge to collapse. As the gorilla falls hundreds of feet to the chasm below, the Boys barely escape, hanging onto the remaining wooden slats as they attempt to climb up to a ledge. Evidently, the footage involving the bomb was shot, but discarded without Laurel's knowledge. Several historians have mentioned that Stan's falling against the keys, without the bomb exploding, makes no sense. In fact, just the contrary seems true as the film is viewed today. Admittedly, having a gorilla wandering about in the Swiss Alps is ludicrous, but it makes as much sense in the comic world of Laurel and Hardy as does a hotel chef planting a bomb in a piano. The scene, involving Stan's drunken stumbling and the menace of the animal, seems far less contrived than a B-film suspense element.

The final scene of *Swiss Miss* features Stan and Ollie departing the hotel for further adventures as mousetrap salesmen. As they are walking down the road in front of the mountain villa, the gorilla reappears, bandaged and on crutches. Swinging one of the crutches above its head, it furiously chases the Boys down the road and into the fade out. In this film, animals cause most of their troubles, with a dog facilitating Stan's drunken state and poor performance on the mountain bridge, and a gorilla finishing them off. This ending is a reworking of the final shot of *The Devil's Brother,* in which a wild bull picks them up and quickly transports them into the Italian countryside.

Another recurring creature, the goat, appears in *Do Detectives Think?* and *Saps at Sea.* In the former, detectives Stan and Ollie are frightened by the shadow of a goat that appears on a cemetery wall. Looming over them, the shadow resembles the conventional image of Satan.

In *Saps at Sea,* a doctor (James Finlayson) orders Ollie to go on an ocean voyage and drink lots of goat's milk. Unable to distinguish between the sexes, the two would-be sailors procure a billy goat and tie him to a dock near their rented boat. When Ollie desires some milk to quiet his nerves, Stan offers to get it for him.

"You know how to milk a goat, don't you?" Ollie asks.

Stan confidently replies, "Sure, just the same as milking a cow. You put the cup in this hand, and take the other hand by the tail and go like that." Moving his right arm up and down, he adds, "Simple."

In a later scene, Stan has put Ollie to sleep by reading him a unique version of the "Old Mother Hubbard" story. Deciding to retire himself, he realizes that the goat, Narcissus, is sound asleep in his bunk. Not wanting to cause any unnecessary noise, Stan climbs into Ollie's narrow bunk, putting his feet directly under his friend's nose. Soon, Ollie wakes, protesting vehemently about Stan's offensive foot odor. Deciding to try his own bunk, Stan climbs in, again placing his head at the foot of the bed. In close-up, the goat shifts violently, sniffs, and quickly exits the cabin.

A more conventional animal menace, the black cat, is featured in several of the early sound shorts. This traditional omen of bad luck scurries across the top of a garden wall in *Night Owls,* causing Stan to land on top of his companion. One of their most unimaginative films, *The Laurel-Hardy Murder Case,* a parody of late 1920s and early 1930s dark house mysteries, features a black cat jumping onto the bed in which the Boys are cowering.

Other animal encounters occur in *Habeas Corpus* (1928), in which a turtle carries off Stan's candle while he is alone in a graveyard, *The Music Box,* with the Boys' horse, Susie, causing a piano to fall on Ollie's back, and *Way Out West,* when the Boys, attempting to use a mule as a boost, send it flying through the side of Mickey Finn's saloon. A lengthy sequence involving a pet ostrich was shot for *Any Old Port,* but was eventually discarded.

The attitude of animals toward Stan and Ollie is best depicted in a scene from *Below Zero.* As they attempt to raise a few cents by playing music in the freezing cold, Stan hears the sound of a coin hitting the bottom of his tin cup. Investigating, the half-frozen vagrant looks into the container, only to find a bird's egg. Retaliating, Stan and Ollie hurl handfuls of snow up at the now airborne animal. The snowballs miss, slapping an apartment inhabitant in the face.

Instead of stating that animals have a supernatural significance in the Laurel and Hardy films, perhaps it would be better to make the claim that they merely are more resourceful and intelligent than Stan and Ollie.

VIII.

The Boys and Women

> "You must understand that, to be married,
> a man must be broad-minded."
> —Ollie, *The Bohemian Girl* (1936)

Many kinds of objects, inanimate and animate, create a great deal of discord between Stan and Ollie, but do not compare with the problems caused by their interactions with other human beings. The Laurel and Hardy world depends on the constructs created between Stan and Ollie, and whenever a third party enters this milieu, serious conflict is inevitable.

Women as characters in the Laurel and Hardy films are never treated very well, which may explain some of the aversion to the team that female viewers have experienced over the years. Feminists have accused Stan and Ollie of being misogynists, and, after a cursory viewing of their films, this conclusion would not be difficult to formulate.

A close examination of the films, however, produces a less simplistic conclusion. Stan and Ollie are not misogynistic—they simply are not able to become involved in a serious relationship with a member of the opposite sex. When a male-female relationship becomes possible for either of them, this behavior threatens the strong bond which has developed between the Boys. If one of them is married, the other lives in the same house, across the hall, or next door. Marriage interrupts the relationship between Stan and Ollie, and this tension inevitably adds friction to the relations between husband and wife.

The wives are always somewhat shrewish, conservative, and demanding. When married, neither Stan nor Ollie experiences much freedom, and demands produced by the wives cut into the time the Boys could be spending together. Ollie is married in several of the

films, while Stan experiences the blessed bonds of matrimony in only a few. When both have wives, twice the pandemonium occurs, but Stan's wife is usually the kindest of the two. There is only one film, *Blotto,* in which only Stan is married.

When Stan has a wife, he pays little attention to her. He rarely utters a word, obviously frightened by a woman who exhibits the mannerisms of a mother trying to repress the desires of her son. Ollie behaves in a similar way, but constantly attempts to communicate with his wife. Charles Barr comments that "he treats his wives, in various films, the way a child acts marriage in play, with sloppy little blown-kisses and simperings."[1]

Their fourth film, *Love 'Em and Weep* (1927), features Stan and Ollie portraying characters who are married, but *Their Purple Moment* is the first film to feature the well-defined "Boys-wives" confrontation. The opening scene shows Stan knocking on the door of his own house, hoping to gain his wife's attention so he may enter. She opens the door, immediately asking him what he has done with his paycheck. Stan gives her the money, but she notices that the amount of three dollars is missing from the usual sum. When Ollie arrives a short time later, he informs Stan that Mrs. Hardy became upset when she noticed that two dollars were absent from his pay packet.

Much like the wives of *Their Purple Moment,* every subsequent spouse is suspicious of her husband's every move, accusing him of every indiscretion imaginable. In *We Faw Down,* both wives see Stan and Ollie jumping out of an apartment window, attempting to pull their pants on. What appears to have been an extramarital affair was actually an innocent escapade. The Boys had fallen into a water puddle, and two women offered to dry their clothes for them. The final nail in the coffin comes when one of the women arrives at the Hardy household to return Ollie's vest. Seeing this, Stan immediately points to his, proving his innocence to his wife. This is to no avail, however, and both wives grab shotguns, chasing the Boys out the door and between apartment buildings. As they shoot, a plethora of unfaithful husbands drop from windows surrounding both sides of the alley.

Opposite: Attempting to picnic with their wives (Kay Deslys, Isabelle Keith) and Uncle Edgar (Edgar Kennedy), the Boys experience a violent altercation with a neighbor (Baldwin Cooke) in *Perfect Day* (1929).

That's My Wife (1929) features a Hardy marriage broken up by Stan. According to Mrs. Hardy, "He dropped in to visit for five minutes, and he's been here for two years. Moreover, he eats grapes in bed." It is obvious that a marriage simply cannot last if a friend drops in to visit for two years, and Mrs. Hardy's complaint about Stan's eating in bed is certainly grounds for divorce. Her comment seems to insinuate that Stan may be sharing the same bed with Ollie and his wife, certainly not the ideal situation for a married couple.

After his wife leaves him, Ollie insists that Stan pose as his wife in order to help him collect an inheritance from a wealthy uncle. Stan reluctantly agrees to dress as a woman and accompany Ollie and Uncle Bernal to the Pink Pup for dining and dancing. Bernal soon discovers the gag, declaring, "I'll leave my money to a dog and cat hospital." Stan also masquerades as a woman, with similar results, in *Why Girls Love Sailors* (1927), *Sugar Daddies, Another Fine Mess, Twice Two,* and *A Chump at Oxford.*

The finest example of the struggle between the Boys and the wives occurs in *Sons of the Desert.* Both Stan and Ollie are married, living in adjacent apartments, with Stan continually coming to visit while his wife is out duck hunting. In the opening scene, the "exhausted ruler" of the Sons of the Desert commands that all members of the sacred fraternal order must attend the national convention in Chicago. Ollie's wife refuses to let him go, forcing him to devise yet another ruse to get out of the house.

Claiming that he is traveling to Honolulu for his health, Ollie takes Stan along so he will have someone to take care of him. Instead, the Boys attend the Chicago bash, drinking champagne and whooping it up with hundreds of members (including Charley Chase). All goes well, including their return to Los Angeles, until the wives hear of the Honolulu cruise ship sinking in a typhoon. Attempting to ease the pain, Mrs. Laurel and Mrs. Hardy attend a local theater and spot their husbands hamming it up in a newsreel film.

The Boys arrive home just before their wives, not knowing of the typhoon disaster. After Ollie notices a newspaper headline, he and Stan hide in the attic, but eventually are forced by the weather to go inside the apartment and come clean. After Ollie lies to both women, Stan relays the actual story to his wife. The last scene involves Stan receiving candy and a drink from his wife, while Ollie suffers an onslaught of flying dishes, pots, and pans from his. The film ends with Stan informing Ollie that "honesty is the best politics."

Block-Heads provides a look at a very well-developed Ollie-wife relationship. In this film, set in 1938, World War I has been over for 20 years, but Stan, unaware that an armistice was ever agreed upon, still guards his trench in France. Not being able to see his companion for this great length of time, Ollie has married, and is celebrating his first wedding anniversary. Far from being a traditional patriarchal household, the Hardy home is depicted, in the very first scene, as being very much in the control of *Mrs.* Hardy (whom, Ollie informs us, owns everything, including the family car). Shown as being very independent, Mrs. Hardy (Minna Gombell) has relegated Ollie to the position of house-husband, who wears an apron and serves her a breakfast of bacon, eggs, and toast. Placing his wife's plate on the table, Ollie sheepishly utters, "I almost burned my finger on the bacon this morning." After being reminded that it is their wedding anniversary, he asks, "Can I have an extra dollar with my allowance today?"

Ollie's most pleasant spouse to appear in the films, Mrs. Hardy, replies, "You may have an extra dollar and twenty-five cents today." Appearing to have a type of mother-and-son relationship, all goes smoothly until Ollie reads a newspaper article telling of his friend being found in a trench on an old French battlefield. Twenty years of separation prove to be too much for Ollie, who quickly forgets about buying his wife an anniversary gift as he rushes to meet Stan at the Old Soldiers' Home. After they are reunited, the joyful Ollie tells Stan, "My home is your home. I'm never going to let you out of my sight again."

Returning to his apartment, Ollie allows Stan to drive the car into the garage, so his friend may see how the automatic door opener operates. Of course, Stan pushes the accelerator to the floor, misses the metal plate on the driveway, and smashes through the door. Minutes later, as the Boys sit in the apartment, Mrs. Hardy returns from shopping, enraged because of the destruction of her car and garage, and refuses to cook a meal for the "knickknack" Ollie has brought home. She then informs Ollie that she is leaving to stay with her mother, inspiring the rejected husband to prepare the food himself. Soon, the stove explodes, wrecking the kitchen.

Block-Heads ends with a recreation of the final sequence from

We Faw Down, showing Ollie and his friend being forcibly ejected from hearth and home. This film solidifies the Laurel and Hardy motif of women consistently having the upper hand, never tolerating the childlike activities of Stan and Ollie, and certainly not allowing themselves to be taken advantage of.

The relationships the two characters experience with their wives provide further evidence for their almost asexual natures. Although the Boys are married in many of the films, a consummation of the matrimonial bond is never apparent. In *Brats,* both Stan and Ollie have sons, but they are not normal human children. Appearing as if they were created through one of Stan's feats of white magic, rather than biological reproduction, "little Stan" and "little Ollie" are midget reproductions of their fathers (resembling the Lilliputians in Swift's *Gulliver's Travels).*

Brats is the only film in which Stan and Ollie have children, although Ollie believes he has a daughter in *The Bohemian Girl.* Ollie's wife (Mae Busch), in order to exact revenge for her lover (Antonio Moreno), who has been beaten by an oppressive count, kidnaps the nobleman's young daughter. When Ollie sees the strange child playing around his gypsy wagon, he is understandably curious. "If you must know, she's yours," replies Mrs. Hardy.

Ollie believes her wholeheartedly, with Stan wishing, "I hope you grow up to be as good a mother as your father." Obviously ignorant of the reproduction process, Ollie's conception of procreation is similar to that of the young child who believes in the stork.

Other mature women whom Stan and Ollie encounter are very similar to the wives. They are usually prostitutes, gangsters' mistresses, or everyday women of the man-hunting variety. The only women who are treated with respect and care are those who are still reasonably young or very old.

Jacqueline Wells (Julie Bishop) portrays young women in both *Any Old Port* and *The Bohemian Girl.* In both films, Stan and Ollie rescue her character from evil older men who intend to force her into marriage or use her as a kidnap victim. *One Good Turn* involves Stan and Ollie's attempt to acquire $100 that an old woman needs to pay her rent. The Boys actually auction off their only possession, a Model T, in order to raise the money. In reality, Stan and Ollie have heard the woman rehearsing for a community play in which a villain (James Finlayson) menaces her for the rent.

These films present an interesting contrast to the wife-oriented productions. Perhaps Stan and Ollie only have respect for the elderly and the innocent type of woman who has yet to become affected by societal institutions such as work and marriage. The Boys cannot function as married persons or become involved with women who require attention, since it would drastically affect their exclusive attraction for each other.

Way Out West includes both "good" and "bad" women who become involved with Stan and Ollie. The plot of the film concerns the Boys' attempt to deliver a gold mining deed to an innocent young woman, Mary Roberts (Rosina Lawrence). The two men become chivalrous in their actions, helping to save the woman, who has been swindled by Mickey Finn (James Finlayson) and his gold digger wife, Lola Marcel (Sharon Lynne). The final scene features the triumphant pair, walking across the plains, with Mary riding atop their beloved mule, Dinah.

Direct visual evidence for the Boys' aversion to women is presented when Lola attempts to wrest the mining deed away from them. The mischievous female pins the retreating Stan to a bed, attempting to tickle him into submission while Mickey Finn chases Ollie around the hotel. The scene is lengthy, reaching the proportions of a comic rape, with Stan hysterically kicking on the bed and laughing himself into a state of near insanity.

The objectivity of *Way Out West* is rarely presented in the Laurel and Hardy world. When female characters are featured, they usually inhabit traditional marriage roles. An early exploration of the Boys' attitude toward marriage occurs in the aptly titled *Should Married Men Go Home?*, which opens with Ollie and his wife cuddling on the couch. As the two lovebirds are enjoying a quiet morning together, the scene cuts outside to Stan, who, dressed for golf, is quickly advancing up the sidewalk toward the Hardy home. Attempting to please Mrs. Hardy, Ollie first feigns disapproval of his friend's arrival and hides behind the front door, but soon his inseparable companion is inside the house, tearing the shades from the windows and wrecking the furniture. After Stan's request to hear "The Maiden's Prayer" prompts the record player to self-destruct, Ollie's wife can stand it no longer, suggesting that her husband join Stan on the golf course. Ollie quickly responds, removing his sweater to reveal his golfing outfit underneath.

Perhaps Stan's understanding of marriage is best summed up by a scene in *Me and My Pal.* It is Ollie's wedding day and Stan has been selected as best man. The prospective bridegroom is sitting anxiously on his sofa when his companion arrives, holding two parcels — a bag of rice and a wrapped box. Unable to wait, Ollie asks what wedding gift Stan has concealed in the box. Stan proudly tears the paper from the package, displaying "Jigsaw Puzzle, Number 86." A dumbfounded Ollie asks, "What did you go and buy a thing like that for?"

Stan replies by stating, "Now that you're going to be married, you won't be going out much at night . . . and this will give us something to play with."

Stan opens the box and begins to put the puzzle together on a coffee table, with Ollie and the butler soon joining in. A short time later, a cab driver, a bicyclist, and a policeman, who have all entered the house for various professional reasons, are also thoroughly engrossed in the mysterious fun. As they are playing, a phone call from Ollie's prospective father-in-law (James Finlayson) is received by Stan. Stan tells him that "Mr. Hardy is right here. He told me to tell you we just left . . . ten minutes ago."

Soon, the bride's father arrives at the Hardy home, and a full-scale battle ensues — Stan's interest in putting together a jigsaw puzzle has escalated into total war. The film ends with the interior of the house completely wrecked and the wedding canceled. In this instance, Stan has destroyed Ollie's marriage before it ever begins.

The content of *Me and My Pal* recalls a similar incident in *Our Wife,* when Stan prevents Ollie from obtaining a wife. Acting as best man, Stan is mistaken for the groom by a cross-eyed justice of the peace (Ben Turpin). After presiding over the ceremony, the justice decides to perform the post-ceremony tradition himself, kissing Ollie instead of the bride. Rather than marrying Dulcy (Julie London) to Ollie, the mixed-up justice bonds Stan and Ollie together. Thoroughly confused, Stan quickly weeps out of self-pity, while Ollie registers an expression of complete disgust.

The most outrageous version of anti-marriage occurs in *Pack Up Your Troubles,* in which the Boys, who are attempting to locate the grandparents of a little girl, disrupt a wedding ceremony. The girl in question is the child of a deceased war buddy, and Stan and Ollie feel it is their duty to find a suitable home for her. After the two men inform the bride's father that they have ... brought Eddie's baby, ... the prospective father-in-law becomes enraged, kicks the groom in the pants, and calls off the wedding. After the proceedings have been canceled, and it is too late to make amends, Mr. Hathaway, whom the Boys believe is Mr. Smith, realizes the mistake and makes a request for his shotgun.

Not only do Stan and Ollie have problems with their own marriages, but they also prohibit others from tying the blessed knot. This tragic scene, along with the one from *Me and My Pal,* is the ultimate expression of the Laurel and Hardy attitude toward marriage.

IX.
The Boys and Society

"Just as I thought ... a couple of crummy,
no-good slackers."—recruiting sergeant,
Pack Up Your Troubles (1932)

Most of the Laurel and Hardy films were produced during the years of the Great Depression, and the social and economic atmosphere of this period pervades many of them. The social status of Stan and Ollie is never the same from one film to the next, and they manage to cover all classes of American society with equal regularity.

In the early 1930s, however, they began to portray themselves as vagrants quite often, getting arrested for sleeping on park benches and playing music in the streets. Stan and Ollie live in the streets at various moments in *You're Darn Tootin', Night Owls, Below Zero, Another Fine Mess, One Good Turn,* and *Scram.*

Below Zero, a minor masterpiece of film technique and performance, contains a large amount of socially relevant material. The narrative is paced very slowly, giving the film an ambience unique to their work: snow is falling, movement of people on the streets is very minimal, and Stan and Ollie sit out in the midst of winter, freezing to death as they attempt to raise a few coins by playing music. Times have gotten so bad that a person, masquerading as a blind man, steals their only dollar.

An eerie atmosphere of silence pervades the film, as there is a complete lack of the usual sounds emanating from automobiles and crowds of people. The only form of employment the Boys can find is performing "The Good Old Summertime" in the freezing winter cold, an act which is not appreciated by other people. One woman becomes so irate that she rubs snow in Ollie's face and smashes their musical instruments.

79

After their livelihood has been destroyed, Stan spots a wallet, lying on the sidewalk, covered with snow. Slowly advancing to pick it up, another down-on-his-luck bum sees it, also. The Boys grab the wallet and run, with the villain close at their heels. Luckily, a policeman intervenes, telling Stan and Ollie that "the neighborhood is filled with thugs and pickpockets who will cut your throat for a dime."

Ollie immediately invites the officer to join them for dinner. Stating that he would like to have something to eat before he gets his throat cut, Stan agrees. The party of three proceeds to Pete's Diner, where they all enjoy huge T-bone steaks and onions. As they are finishing their meal, bouncers begin to strike a customer and throw him out the door. Becoming curious, the policeman consults the head waiter, Pete (Stanley Sandford), who answers that it was "just a bozo who couldn't pay the check."

"Imagine being in a predicament like that," Ollie happily quips to the policeman, insisting that he and his friend pay the check. Stan opens the wallet to extract some of the huge amount of cash within, noticing that the identification photo is that of their pal, the police officer. Stan is dazed long enough to allow the cop to spot his wallet and grab it from him. Without consulting them first, he accuses Stan and Ollie of being cheap pickpockets, stating that they will get ten years for this criminal act. Instead of letting the law take its course, the officer leaves them at the mercy of Pete and his own distinct brand of vigilante violence.

The angered waiter grabs Ollie, tossing him out the back door and into the street, where he is almost struck by a speeding automobile. Stan receives the worst of the treatment, being thrown into a barrel of ice-covered water. This scene reaches near horrific proportions, as sounds of gurgling water fill the soundtrack. Ollie walks over toward the building, loudly asking the whereabouts of his companion. Lifting the lid from the barrel, he discovers Stan inside, hiccoughing, stating that he has drunk all of the water. Tipping the barrel over, Stan rolls out, his stomach swollen to balloon-sized proportions. Jumping up and down, he quickly whispers something into Ollie's ear, and the two run into the fade out.

Below Zero presents indirect commentary on the evils of the Depression — jobs are not to be found, and, when a meal can be procured, fascistic proprietors beat their patrons senseless and leave them to die in the cold. The only policeman in the film has a wallet

The Boys publicly humiliate Kennedy (Edgar Kennedy) in *Leave 'Em Laughing* (1928).

bulging with money, while Stan, physically handicapped, and Ollie have not been able to acquire a cent.

In *Saps at Sea* (a film including scenes reminiscent of Chaplin's *Modern Times*), the Boys also find it difficult to maintain a job because of the strain modern methods are imposing upon the industrial workplace. Stan and Ollie are "horn testers" at the Sharp and Pierce Horn and Manufacturing Company who witness their fellow workers going insane under the pressures of labor. Soon, the horns take their toll on Ollie, who experiences a nervous breakdown and is diagnosed as having "hornophobia."

More than any other classic comedians, Laurel and Hardy constantly undermine authority figures and professional people. Policemen are their favorite target, receiving such "dignified" treatment as being depantsed, backed over by cars, hit on the head, and other various forms of public humiliation.

In *Sugar Daddies,* Stan, being harassed by an officer, grabs the cap from his head and tosses it into the street. In *The Second One Hundred Years,* a policeman stands idly by as the Boys, disguised as painters, splatter whitewash all over parked cars, while a crusading cop in *The Battle of the Century* gets a swift pie in the face.

"Kennedy" (Edgar Kennedy) is the character to appear most often as a policeman, exercising too much power and receiving his just rewards each time. In *Leave 'Em Laughing,* Stan orders him to crank their Model T and cuts the belt from his pants as both "offenders" laugh hysterically. Ollie backs over him with the car, and, when Kennedy insists that he drive the Boys out of the mess, he twice hits an auto behind them, creates yet another mammoth traffic jam, and finishes them off by sinking the car into a muddy construction site.

Kennedy is almost annihilated in *The Finishing Touch,* in which he first appears on the scene, telling them, "If you must make a noise, make it quietly," and kicking Stan in the rear end. At various points in the narrative, Kennedy is hit on the head, knocked to the ground, given a black eye by a nurse, and covered with white paint, roofing glue, and shingles. Most of the cop bashing comes unknowingly from Ollie, since Kennedy frequently happens to be in the vicinity of one of Ollie's mistakes.

Other policemen receive even worse treatment in many of the films. A motorcycle patrolman has his vehicle completely crushed by a truck in *Two Tars,* a cop-on-the-beat gets beaten by a housewife's rug and smashed down to dwarf-like proportions in *Liberty,* and yet another officer gets shot in the rear end by a millionaire in *Wrong Again.* Walking into the wealthy man's home, he exclaims, "This man almost blew my brains out!"

Almost every film contains at least one policeman getting his comeuppance, and it is usually stressed that the public official truly deserves this kind of treatment. Police in the Laurel and Hardy world are constantly oppressive, making ridiculous demands for reasonably miniscule crimes. In *Night Owls,* Kennedy finds Stan and Ollie asleep on a park bench, threatening to "give them 90 days on the rock pile."

An even more extreme punishment is dealt to the Boys in the final scene of *The Midnight Patrol* (1933), in which they both have jobs *as* policemen. Having mistakenly arrested the chief of police, the enraged official grabs a pistol, marches them into an off-screen cell, and guns them down in cold blood.

Judges are depicted in a similar light, with Judge Beaumont (Rychard Cramer) in *Scram* first running the Boys out of town and then shooting at them in the final scene. A judge in *Our Relations* makes bizarre hand gestures toward Stan and Ollie, appearing to be competely insane.

Military men have been used as comic foils almost as long as cinema has existed. Like policemen and judges, military commanders are also depicted as ruthless, inhuman beasts in the Laurel and Hardy films. Beginning with *With Love and Hisses* in 1927 and ending with *The Flying Deuces* in 1939, the military is frequently used as a device in the Laurel and Hardy canon. In films such as *Two Tars* and *Men o' War* (1929), Stan and Ollie are dressed in military uniforms, but are involved in civilian matters.

In the several films in which they are actually members of a military unit, the Boys are unable to perform any type of organized drill or routine. This deficiency certainly stems from the coordination problems they have, but it also helps them to maintain their individuality.

One of the reasons that Stan and Ollie are so inept at military routine is the fact that neither of them has any idea how the military functions or is able to comprehend even the most rudimentary commands. When first arriving at the Foreign Legion barracks in *Beau*

Hunks, Stan inquires, "Can we get a room by ourselves?" Ollie has no conception of the process of military rank, calling the camp commandant (Charles Middleton) several erroneous titles, including "admiral."

The Boys participate in World War I in *Pack up Your Troubles.* In the midst of battle, an officer hopes to rid himself of Stan and Ollie by ordering them to secure a German stronghold. Much to his surprise, they blunder into a tank, advance across enemy lines, corral an entire unit of Germans, and bring them back to their own trench.

In *Bonnie Scotland,* after joining the British army, they participate in a marching exercise. Stan is unable to get into proper step, but all the other soldiers, accustomed to conformity, gradually adopt Stan's method, until the entire regiment follows suit.

In *The Flying Deuces,* the Boys decide that they have had their fill of the Foreign Legion and prepare to leave. Ollie writes a note to the commandant, informing him of their departure, not realizing that enlistment is measured in *years,* not days, of service.

These scenes indicate the extent to which Stan and Ollie are "abnormal" human beings. Much like their ability to escape harm in the tit-for-tat incidents, they can also walk through modern warfare without obtaining a scratch. None of the military organizations are capable of indoctrinating them, but the Boys are capable of changing the routines of the military by using their own haphazard methods.

Other organized groups are also disrupted by the actions of Stan and Ollie. The opening scene of *Sons of the Desert* features a formal meeting of "The Sons of the Desert," a Shriner-type organization. While the "exhausted ruler" lectures to a large crowd of Sons, a knock is heard at the back of the room. The speech halts, as the door opens and the Boys fumble their way into the room, tripping over chairs and falling into the laps of disgusted members. Even before the plot of the film has been established, Stan and Ollie display their inability to conform to societal procedures.

Another major authority figure is the landlord, a character whom the Boys must frequently do business with. Charlie Hall appears as an unreasonable apartment house owner in several films, always threatening to evict them and using physical violence to stress his point. *Leave 'Em Laughing, They Go Boom* (1929), and *Laughing Gravy* all feature sequences which include a pants-kicking or similar contest between Stan and Ollie and the Hall landlord. In *Laughing*

Gravy, the Boys present such an infinite problem, coupled with a smallpox quarantine, that it forces the landlord to commit suicide by shooting himself.

A landlord played by Edgar Kennedy in *Angora Love* is so severe that he prompts Ollie to describe him to Stan as "a killer." Telling Stan to be quiet, he adds, "That landlord will assassinate us." When Stan and Ollie create a disturbance a short time later, the killer rips through the door, yelling, "Send a cop! There's gonna be a murder!"

The bourgeois shop- or homeowner is also attacked with a vengeance, beginning in the early silent films, and continuing to hold this "honored" position until the late 1930s. Again, it is Charlie Hall who experiences a great deal of abuse, having thousands of his pies destroyed in *The Battle of the Century* and his gumball machines smashed in *Two Tars.*

James Finlayson frequently appears as a shopkeeper or innocent homeowner. Owning a music store in *Liberty,* he experiences the destruction of a gramophone, dozens of records, and a harmonium, while his home in *Big Business* is viciously attacked and decimated by Stan and Ollie. In *A Chump at Oxford,* Finlayson, who has hired the two incompetents as servants at a society gathering, is called "the old guy" by Ollie and has his party turned into a free-for-all within minutes.

Leaving no class unscathed, the Boys constantly poke fun at high-class society individuals. In *The Second One Hundred Years,* they refuse to bow to a group of society women, choosing to crudely shake hands with them instead, and a wealthy woman is isolated from the rest of the crowd in tight close-up just before she is pummeled with a pie in *The Battle of the Century.*

Society males get a thrashing in *Wrong Again,* when Ollie tosses hay into a man's face and knocks the wheel from another's horse cart. Later in the film, when Stan is attempting to understand the behavior of a certain socialite, Ollie informs him that "these millionaires think just the reverse of other people."

Another Fine Mess features James Finlayson as Colonel Wilburforce Buckshot, millionaire and big game hunter. After Buckshot departs for a hunting excursion to South Africa, Stan and Ollie duck into his cellar in an effort to escape from a policeman. When a wealthy British couple arrives to rent the estate, the Boys are forced to impersonate the members of the Buckshot household. Ollie's portrayal of the Colonel is tinged with pomposity and extravagance, and he treats the butler and maid (both played by Stan) like dogs. The final scene involves Colonel Buckshot returning home, grabbing a shotgun, and, aided by policemen, chasing Stan and Ollie out of his house.

Royalty is trampled underfoot in *Double Whoopee* (1929), in which the pretentiousness of a visiting prince is completely undermined by Stan and Ollie. The Prince, a parody of Erich von Stroheim's "Teutonic Aristocrats," arrives at an American hotel where the Boys have been employed as valets. On three separate occasions, Stan and Ollie cause his highness to fall into a greasy elevator shaft, ruining his expensive uniform each time. The last fall also involves the Prime Minister, who lands on top of his boss.

The Bohemian Girl also features a major figure of royalty, Count Arnheim (William P. Carlton), a selfish and frequently vicious authoritarian. Stan and Ollie are members of a Bohemian gypsy band who attempt to earn an "honest" living by telling fortunes and picking pockets. The entire troupe is ordered to leave the count's domain and several members are captured and tortured by his henchmen. In the final scene of the film, Arnheim orders his police force to flog his own daughter (whom he does not recognize due to many years of separation) "within an inch of her life." Evil triumphs in this film, however, with the daughter returning to the oppressive father and the Boys being brutally tortured and disfigured.

Professional men and scholars are depicted as being nothing but pretentious individuals, bordering on insanity. A scientist in *Habeas Corpus,* who theorizes that "the brain has a level surface ... in some instances, practically flat," uses his vest pocket as an ashtray and hires Stan and Ollie to provide him with corpses for his experiments.

The Music Box provides the most extreme example of the behavior of a scholar, with Billy Gilbert essaying the role of Professor Theodore von Schwarzenhoffen, M.D., A.D., D.D.S., F.L.D., F.F.F., und F. As the Boys attempt to carry the heavy piano up the steps, Schwarzenhoffen approaches from above, banging on the crate, demanding that they get out of the way. Refusing to walk around, he informs them that, if they do not move, he will "commit murder."

A parody of horror films that were popular during the period, *Dirty Work* (1933) offers Professor Noodle, a mad scientist who has discovered the secret of the "rejuvenation of life." Noodle relishes working with chemicals, cutting a liquid drop in half with scissors and frequently quacking like a duck as he labors. Finally, experimenting on a duck, he develops a formula which actually makes organisms much younger. In the final scene, the scientist departs to look for a human subject, leaving the Boys alone in his laboratory. Stan is curious to see if the experiment actually works, deciding to try it on a fish and enlisting Ollie as his assistant. While searching for an eyedropper, Stan knocks Ollie and the serum into a huge water vat in the center of the room. The water churns and foams violently, until a chimpanzee emerges, speaking in Ollie's voice. Stan stares at the devolved Ollie, and begins to cry.

Stan himself becomes a scholar in *A Chump at Oxford*. When he and Ollie arrive at the venerable institution, a valet refers to Stan as Lord Paddington, a famous student and athlete who, after having a window shut on his head, lost his memory and disappeared, "never to be heard from again." Later, when Stan is looking out the window, it comes slamming down onto his head, nearly knocking him unconscious. After regaining his senses, he begins talking in a preposterous and highbrow fashion, causing the valet to rejoice that "Lord Paddington has returned."

As Lord Paddington, Stan becomes insufferable, making Ollie his lackey and offering to give advice to Einstein, who "needs to be straightened out on his theory." Fortunately, in the final scene, he receives another hit by the window, transforming him back into the real Stan. Ollie, who has threatened to walk out on him, is thrilled that his old friend has come back.

You're Darn Tootin' includes two scenes of Stan and Ollie humiliating an orchestra conductor. Near the beginning of the film, Stan, playing a clarinet, blasts the musician's hat from his head. When the man steps down to retrieve it, he trips over the podium, rolling down to join the hat on the ground. A later scene, featuring a double humiliation, has the Boys blurting out a horrible melody on a sidewalk below the conductor's rehearsal room. The conductor grabs the tank from a water cooler and pours it out the window, soaking a policeman where Stan and Ollie had been standing moments before.

Pack Up Your Troubles not only features the frustration of military commanders, but a full-scale assault on every conceivable figure of authority. Policemen, the wealthy, a welfare agent, and a bank president are all characters who receive their just rewards at the hands of Stan and Ollie. In one scene, the bank president agrees to loan them "a couple of thousand" when he thinks that the Boys own a chain of restaurant businesses. After he discovers that they only possess a small lunch wagon, he laughs, stating, "I'd have to be unconscious to loan you money on *that*." As soon as these words are spoken, a bust of William Shakespeare topples from its pedestal, knocking him unconscious. Taking the president on his word, Stan and Ollie walk into the vault, withdraw two thousand dollars, and flee the bank.

No group of people is sacred in the Laurel and Hardy films, as the Boys, with their alternative relationship, are the only persons who, in the final analysis, are likeable human beings. When they are involved in a dyadic encounter that contains violence, they are able to forgive one another, but, if other persons are involved, the conflict escalates to a state of complete anarchy. No matter how advanced a person may be in the eyes of society, all human beings are reduced to the same level in the Laurel and Hardy films. Even those films which feature Stan and Ollie as middle- or upper-class citizens show them humiliated and disillusioned in the final frames.

Not only a sense of humiliation, but outright injury, befalls the Boys in the films in which they choose to aid authority figures. In *Going Bye-Bye* (1934), Stan and Ollie provide evidence which sends notorious criminal Butch Long (Walter Long) to prison. Vowing revenge, Butch escapes from the law only a day later. Seeking out the Boys, he attacks them, "wrapping their legs around their necks."

The Live Ghost (1934) features Stan and Ollie as assistants to a domineering sea captain (Walter Long), who, after discovering that the Boys have broken one of his laws, turns their heads a total of one hundred and eighty degrees, so that "when they're walking north, they'll be facing south."

The final moments of *The Bohemian Girl,* in which Stan and Ollie are tortured, include the two abused vagrants walking out of Count Arnheim's dungeon in a very painful predicament—Stan has been crushed to dwarf size, while Ollie has been stretched on the rack to a gigantic length. These incidents of physical distortion represent an exaggerated view of the Boys' inability to exist within the boundaries of conventional society.

Charles Barr claims that

> it is in their characters to be stupid enough, and tolerant enough, to wipe the slate clean after each encounter. They do not learn and they do not, for long, resent. But pain is by no means anaesthetized. Few actors suffer so vividly as (in particular) Ollie, or transfer their pain so fully to the audience. The films are highly therapeutic in letting us repeatedly indulge our violent urges but making us laugh at and judge them at the same time. They are the clearest illustration of the Aristotelian idea of purging.[1]

In his 1973 book, *The Comic Mind*, Gerald Mast comments on this aspect of the Laurel and Hardy relationship: "Not only are Stan and Ollie nasty children in their incompetence and spitefulness, but the world itself in their films is populated solely with brats. The childish spite of the central pair runs up against the equally childish spite of their opponents."[2]

Mast's observations are interesting and informative, but he misses one essential point—a person must be something other than a child in order to exhibit child*ish* behavior. Since Stan and Ollie's mental capacities are retarded to a great degree, they *are* overgrown children, and thus, their behavior is child*like*, not child*ish*.

Mast claims that the behavior of Stan and Ollie transforms normal people into "a mass of pie-slingers, shin-kickers, and pants-pullers."[3] He also claims that all the other characters in the films are "brats." This is a much too superficial analysis, as one merely needs to observe how adults act around children to notice what is happening in the Laurel and Hardy world. Many characters appear respectable in their roles in adult society until Stan and Ollie appear on the scene. The behavior that ultimately results is not unlike the way an adult responds to the babbling and irrational activity of young children.

The insanity which usually develops (destruction of property, kicking, slapping) is a product of childlike play. The Boys really have no clearly defined idea of what type of behavior is socially acceptable and they continue to delight in a crazed mode of play. No one actually remains injured, however humiliated they may appear to be. When Stan and Ollie continue exhibiting this behavior, it seems logical, since they are still considered to be children. When the surrounding adults continue, however, they look absurd and foolish.

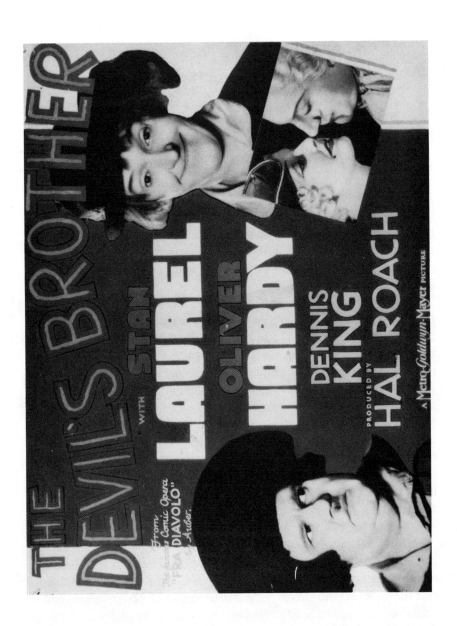

Frequently, it is the father figure of the policeman who stifles Stan and Ollie's behavior at the end of films.

The depiction of normal people in the Laurel and Hardy milieu is particularly interesting in *Bonnie Scotland,* which features an entire subplot including characters who never interact with Stan and Ollie — a device which provides a look at "typical" human beings. An aspect which has been criticized for weakening the narrative of the film, these characters (including a society woman, a young heiress, and an army colonel) appear as if they are a parody of most civilized people — individuals who have become conventionalized, boring, and lethargic. Only Stan and Ollie appear to be interesting, and if *Bonnie Scotland* is viewed from this perspective, their scenes appear to be even more humorous and engaging — the acquisition of a hotel room, the frying of a fish, and the removal of litter become fascinating when performed by these two men.

The Devil's Brother provides the perfect summation of the Laurel and Hardy world view. Their alternative lifestyle is the only "correct" one in this film, as they are surrounded by unfaithfulness and corruption on all sides. "Stanlio" and Ollio" experience a warm father-and-son type of relationship in this film, while other characters find nothing but falsity.

The relationship between Lord Rocburg (James Finlayson) and Lady Pamela Rocburg (Thelma Todd) is so bad that it encourages her to lust after Fra Diavolo, who, interested only in her jewels, feigns love for the Lady. Zerlina (Lucille Browne) is deeply in love with Lorenzo (Arthur Pierson), an impoverished soldier, but her uncaring father, Matteo (Henry Armetta), is forcing her into a marriage with an unattractive but wealthy fop. The only characters in the film who attempt to work together for a common purpose are Stanlio and Ollio.

The Stan and Ollie partnership endures because of its deviation from the status quo. Their relationship, like many of the events and gag structures in the films, is successful solely because of its unconventionality. By utilizing an almost surreal style of exaggeration and outrageousness, Laurel and Hardy encourage us to examine the reality of our own irrational world.

Opposite: Laurel and Hardy, as they appear in the poster advertising for *The Devil's Brother* (1933).

X.
Filmography:
The Roach Period
(1926–1940)

Included here is a complete filmography of the films Laurel and Hardy made while under contract to Hal Roach. The analyses in the earlier chapters pertain to these films, which constitute the true Laurel and Hardy canon. The filmography of *The Flying Deuces* (1939), produced at RKO Studios, may be found in the next chapter, which deals with the post–Roach films.

The Hal Roach–Laurel and Hardy films maintain a continuity of physical and psychological development from one film to the next, due not only to the constant presence of Stan and Ollie, but to a continuity of production personnel, as well. Most of the individuals who directed the films, such as James Parrott, James W. Horne, Charles Rogers, Lewis Foster, and George Marshall, each helmed several, helping to maintain a consistent level of characterization and quality.

Cameramen and editors also contributed to this smooth process, with individuals such as George Stevens and Art Lloyd photographing a great number of the shorts and features, and two men, Richard Currier and Bert Jordan, editing almost all of them. The extensive Roach stock company of actors, including James Finlayson, Billy Gilbert, Charlie Hall, Stanley (Tiny) Sandford, and Mae Busch, also adds an atmosphere that continues from one story to the next. With this level of professional familiarity being created in both production and post-production areas of operation, the Laurel and Hardy "world" was able to become stabilized as a very well-defined cinematic space.

The actual stabilizing element during the Roach period was undoubtedly the creative presence of Stan Laurel. Supervising the entire filmmaking process, Laurel exercised final approval of Roach's directorial choices, participated in the writing of stories, gags, and dialogue, oversaw the editing, and often guided the decisions of the director. The development of the two complex characters of Stan and Ollie was also facilitated by Laurel and Hardy during production, since they frequently disregarded the written script, choosing to improvise much of their material.

The date presented next to each film title is the date of release. The dates when the film was actually produced are also featured in the credits. The early Laurel and Hardy films were completed for Pathé distribution. In 1927, Hal Roach negotiated distribution rights with Metro-Goldwyn-Mayer, while still owing a few titles to Pathé. Due to some of the MGM films being released before the remaining Pathé titles were shown in theaters, and a few silent shorts being made for theaters not yet equipped for sound, the production chronology differs from the release chronology.

Each listing in the filmography includes a rating (on a scale of one to ten) for overall quality. This rating applies to the films within the Laurel and Hardy canon only, and should not be compared with other similar systems. Also included is a code for each film, which will help in describing the state of Stan and Ollie's relationsip within each narrative. A key for this code is listed below.

Key:

LT — living together	B3 — both against a third party
LS — living separately	BS — both against society
SM — Stan married	CO — comic opera
OM — Ollie married	SS — slapstick material
BM — both married	SE — subtle elements
SO — Stan against Ollie	(nonslapstick in nature)

45 Minutes from Hollywood (December 26, 1926). Code: (Laurel and Hardy do not appear together); rating: 3 (silent). *Directed by* Fred L. Guiol; *produced by* Hal Roach; *story by* Hal Roach; *titles by* H.M. Walker. Filmed August 1926. Running time: 20 minutes. *Cast:* Glen Tryon, Charlotte Mineau, Rube Clifford, Sue O'Neil/Molly O'Day, Theda Bara, the Our Gang Kids, Oliver Hardy, Edna Murphy, Jerry

Mandy, Ham Kinsey, Ed Brandenberg, Jack Hill, Stan Laurel, Al Hallet, Stanley (Tiny) Sandford, the Hal Roach Bathing Beauties.

Duck Soup (March 13, 1927). Code: LT/BS/SS (silent); rating: (film unavailable). *Directed by* Fred L. Guiol; *produced by* Hal Roach; *story by* Arthur J. Jefferson (Stan Laurel's father); *titles by* H.M. Walker. Filmed September 1926. Running time: 20 minutes. *Cast:* Stan Laurel, Madeline Hurlock, Oliver Hardy, William Austin, Bob Kortman. (Note: This film was remade as *Another Fine Mess* in 1930.)

Slipping Wives (April 3, 1927). Code: LS/SO/SS (silent); rating: 2. *Directed by* Fred L. Guiol and Lewis R. Foster; *produced by* Hal Roach; *story by* Hal Roach; *titles by* H.M. Walker; *photographed by* George Stevens; *edited by* Richard Currier. Filmed October 1926. Running time: 20 minutes. *Cast:* Priscilla Dean, Herbert Rawlinson, Stan Laurel, Oliver Hardy, Albert Conti.

Love 'Em and Weep (June 12, 1927). Code: LS/SS (silent); rating: 5. *Directed by* Fred L. Guiol; *produced by* Hal Roach; *story by* Hal Roach; *titles by* H.M. Walker. Filmed January 1927. Running time: 20 minutes. *Cast:* Mae Busch, Stan Laurel, James Finlayson, Oliver Hardy, Charlotte Mineau, Vivien Oakland, Charlie Hall, May Wallace, Ed Brandenberg, Gale Henry. (Note: This film was remade as *Chickens Come Home* in 1931.)

Why Girls Love Sailors (July 17, 1927). Code: LS/SS (silent); rating: 5. *Directed by* Fred L. Guiol; *produced by* Hal Roach; *story by* Hal Roach; *titles by* H.M. Walker. Filmed February 1927. Running time: 20 minutes. *Cast:* Stan Laurel, Oliver Hardy, Bobby Dunn, Sojin, Anna May Wong, Eric Mayne.

With Love and Hisses (August 28, 1927). Code: LS/SS (silent); rating: 7. *Directed by* Fred L. Guiol; *produced by* Hal Roach; *story by* Hal Roach; *titles by* H.M. Walker. Filmed March 1927. Running time: 20 minutes. *Cast:* Stan Laurel, Oliver Hardy, James Finlayson, Frank Brownlee, Chet Brandenberg, Anita Garvin, Eve Southern, Will Stanton, Jerry Mandy, Frank Saputo, Josephine Dunn.

Sugar Daddies (September 10, 1927). Code: LS/B3/SS (silent); rating: 5. *Directed by* Fred L. Guiol; *produced by* Hal Roach; *titles by* H.M. Walker; *photographed by* George Stevens. Filmed June 1927.

Running time: 17 minutes. *Cast:* James Finlayson, Stan Laurel, Oliver Hardy, Noah Young, Charlotte Mineau, Edna Marian, Eugene Pallette, Jack Hill, Charlie Hall, Sam Lufkin, Dorothy Coburn, Ray Cooke, Jiggs (dog).

Sailors, Beware! (September 25, 1927). Code: LS/SS (silent); rating: 5. *Directed by* Hal Yates; *produced by* Hal Roach; *story by* Hal Roach; *titles by* H.M. Walker. Filmed April 1927. Running time: 20 minutes. *Cast:* Stan Laurel, Oliver Hardy, Anita Garvin, Stanley (Tiny) Sandford, Viola Richard, May Wallace, Connie Evans, Barbara Pierce, Lupe Velez, Will Stanton, Ed Brandenberg, Dorothy Coburn, Frank Brownlee, Harry Earles, Charley Young.

The Second One Hundred Years (October 8, 1927). Code: LT/BS/SS/SE (silent); rating: 8. *Directed by* Fred L. Guiol; *produced by* Hal Roach; *titles by* H.M. Walker; *edited by* Richard Currier. Filmed June 1927. Running time: 20 minutes. *Cast:* Stan Laurel, Oliver Hardy, James Finlayson, Eugene Pallette, Stanley (Tiny) Sandford, Ellinor Van Der Veer, Alfred Fisher, Charles A. Bachman, Edgar Deering, Otto Fries, Bob O'Conor, Frank Brownlee, Dorothy Coburn, Charlie Hall, Rosemary Theby.

Call of the Cuckoos (October 15, 1927). Code: LT/B3/SS (silent); rating: 3. *Directed by* Clyde A. Bruckman; *produced by* Hal Roach; *supervised by* Leo McCarey; *titles by* H.M. Walker; *photographed by* Floyd Jackman; *edited by* Richard Currier. Filmed June 1927. Running time: 20 minutes. *Cast:* Max Davidson, Lillian Elliot, Spec O'Donnell, Charley Chase, Stan Laurel, Oliver Hardy, James Finlayson, Frank Brownlee, Charlie Hall, Charles Meakin, Leo Willis, Lyle Tayo, Edgar Dearing, Fay Holderness, Otto H. Fries.

Hats Off (November 5, 1927). Code: LT/B3/SS/SE (silent); rating: (film unavailable). *Directed by* Hal Yates; *produced by* Hal Roach; *supervised by* Leo McCarey; *titles by* H.M. Walker; *edited by* Richard Currier. Filmed July 1927. Running time: 20 minutes. *Cast:* Stan Laurel, Oliver Hardy, James Finlayson, Anita Garvin, Dorothy Coburn, Ham Kinsey, Sam Lufkin, Chet Brandenberg. (Note: No print of this film is known to exist. It was remade as *The Music Box* in 1932.)

Do Detectives Think? (November 20, 1927). Code: LT/B3/SS (silent); rating: 6. *Directed by* Fred L. Guiol; *produced by* Hal Roach;

story by Hal Roach; *titles by* H.M. Walker. Filmed May 1927. Running time: 20 minutes. *Cast:* Stan Laurel, Oliver Hardy, James Finlayson, Viola Richard, Noah Young, Frank Brownlee, Will Stanton, Charley Young, Charles A. Bachman.

Putting Pants on Philip (December 3, 1927). Code: LT/SO/SS (silent); rating: 8. *Directed by* Clyde A. Bruckman; *produced by* Hal Roach; *supervised by* Leo McCarey; *titles by* H.M. Walker; *photographed by* George Stevens; *edited by* Richard Currier. Filmed August 1927. Running time: 20 minutes. *Cast:* Stan Laurel, Oliver Hardy, Sam Lufkin, Harvey Clark, Ed Brandenberg, Dorothy Coburn, Chet Brandenberg, Retta Palmer, Bob O'Conor, Eric Mack, Jack Hill, Don Bailey, Alfred Fisher, Lee Phelps, Charles A. Bachman.

The Battle of the Century (December 31, 1927). Code: LT/BS/SS/SE (silent); rating: 8. *Directed by* Clyde A Bruckman and Hal Roach; *produced by* Hal Roach; *supervised by* Leo McCarey; *story by* Hal Roach; *titles by* H.M. Walker; *photographed by* George Stevens; *edited by* Richard Currier. Filmed September 1927. Running time: 15 minutes. *Cast:* Stan Laurel, Oliver Hardy, Dick Gilbert, George K. French, Dick Sutherland, Sam Lufkin, Noah Young, Gene Morgan, Al Hallet, Anita Garvin, Eugene Pallette, Lyle Tayo, Charlie Hall, Dorothy Coburn, Ham Kinsey, Bert Roach, Jack Hill, Bob O'Conor, Ed Brandenberg, Dorothy Walbert, Charley Young, Ellinor Van Der Veer. (Note: No complete print of *The Battle of the Century* is known to exist. Existing prints feature the complete boxing match, a reconstructed midsection [using stills], and the closing pie fight sequence [which includes original footage and still reproductions].)

Leave 'Em Laughing (January 28, 1928). Code: LT/SO/BS/SS/SE (silent); rating: 7. *Directed by* Clyde A. Bruckman; *produced by* Hal Roach; *supervised by* Leo McCarey; *story by* Hal Roach; *titles by* H.M. Walker; *photographed by* George Stevens; *edited by* Richard Currier. Filmed October 1927. Running time: 20 minutes. *Cast:* Stan Laurel, Oliver Hardy, Edgar Kennedy, Charlie Hall, Viola Richard, Dorothy Coburn, Stanley (Tiny) Sandford, Sam Lufkin, Edgar Dearing, Al Hallet, Jack V. Lloyd, Otto Fries, Jack Hill.

Flying Elephants (February 12, 1928). Code: LS/SO/SS (silent); rating: 5. *Directed by* Fred Butler and Hal Roach; *produced by* Hal Roach; *story by* Hal Roach; *titles by* H.M. Walker. Filmed May 1927.

Running time: 20 minutes. *Cast:* Stan Laurel, Oliver Hardy, James Finlayson, Dorothy Coburn, Leo Willis, Stanley (Tiny) Sandford, Bud Fine.

The Finishing Touch (February 25, 1928). Code: LT/B3/SS (silent); rating: 7. *Directed by* Clyde A. Bruckman; *produced by* Hal Roach; *supervised by* Leo McCarey; *titles by* H.M. Walker; *photographed by* George Stevens; *edited by* Richard Currier. Filmed November 1927. Running time: 20 minutes. *Cast:* Stan Laurel, Oliver Hardy, Edgar Kennedy, Dorothy Coburn, Sam Lufkin.

From Soup to Nuts (March 24, 1928). Code: LT/B3/SS (silent); rating: 7. *Directed by* E. Livingston (Edgar) Kennedy; *produced by* Hal Roach; *supervised by* Leo McCarey; *story by* Leo McCarey; *titles by* H.M. Walker; *photographed by* Len Powers; *edited by* Richard Currier. Filmed December 1927. Running time: 20 minutes. *Cast:* Stan Laurel, Oliver Hardy, Anita Garvin, Stanley (Tiny) Sandford, Otto Fries, Edna Marian, Ellinor Van Der Veer, George Bichel, Dorothy Coburn, Sam Lufkin, Gene Morgan, Buddy (dog).

You're Darn Tootin' (April 21, 1928). Code: LT/SO/B3/BS/SS (silent); rating: 8. *Directed by* E. Livingston (Edgar) Kennedy; *produced by* Hal Roach; *supervised by* Leo McCarey; *titles by* H.M. Walker; *photographed by* Floyd Jackman; *edited by* Richard Currier. Filmed January 1928. Running time: 20 minutes. *Cast:* Stan Laurel, Oliver Hardy, Sam Lufkin, Chet Brandenberg, Christian Frank, Rolfe Sedan, George Rowe, Agnus Steele, Ham Kinsey, William Irving, Charlie Hall, Otto Lederer, Dick Gilbert, Frank Saputo.

Their Purple Moment (May 19, 1928). Code: LS/BM/B3/SS/SE (silent); rating: 8. *Directed by* James Parrott; *produced by* Hal Roach; *supervised by* Leo McCarey; *titles by* H.M. Walker; *photographed by* George Stevens; *edited by* Richard Currier. Filmed February 1928. Running time: 20 minutes. *Cast:* Stan Laurel, Oliver Hardy, Anita Garvin, Kay Deslys, Jimmy Aubrey, Fay Holderness, Lyle Tayo, Leo Willis, Jack Hill, Retta Palmer, Stanley (Tiny) Sandford, Sam Lufkin, Ed Brandenberg, Patsy O'Byrne, Harry Earles.

Should Married Men Go Home? (September 8, 1928). Code: LS/OM/BS/SS/SE (silent); rating: 7. *Directed by* James Parrott; *produced by* Hal Roach; *supervised by* Leo McCarey; *story by* Leo McCarey and James Parrott; *titles by* H.M. Walker; *photographed by* George Stevens;

edited by Richard Currier. Filmed March 13–21, 1928. Running time: 20 minutes. *Cast:* Stan Laurel, Oliver Hardy, Edgar Kennedy, Edna Marian, Viola Richard, John Aassen, Jack Hill, Dorothy Coburn, Lyle Tayo, Chet Brandenberg, Sam Lufkin, Charlie Hall, Kay Deslys.

Early to Bed (October 6, 1928). Code: LT/SO/SS (silent); rating: 8. *Directed by* Emmett Flynn; *produced by* Hal Roach; *supervised by* Leo McCarey; *titles by* H.M. Walker; *photographed by* George Stevens; *edited by* Richard Currier. Filmed May 21–29, 1928. Running time: 20 minutes. *Cast:* Stan Laurel, Oliver Hardy.

Two Tars (November 3, 1928). Code: LT/BS/SS (silent); rating: 10. *Directed by* James Parrott; *produced by* Hal Roach; *supervised by* Leo McCarey; *story by* Leo McCarey; *titles by* H.M. Walker; *photographed by* George Stevens; *edited by* Richard Currier. Filmed June 22–23 and June 26–July 3, 1928. Running time: 20 minutes. *Cast:* Stan Laurel, Oliver Hardy, Thelma Hill, Ruby Blaine, Charley Rogers, Edgar Kennedy, Clara Guiol, Jack Hill, Charlie Hall, Edgar Dearing, Harry Bernard, Sam Lufkin, Baldwin Cooke, Charles McMurphy, Ham Kinsey, Lyle Tayo, Lon Poff, Retta Palmer, George Rowe, Chet Brandenberg, Fred Holmes, Dorothy Walbert, Frank Ellis, Helen Gilmore.

Habeas Corpus (December 1, 1928). Code: LT/B3/SS (silent); rating: 6. *Directed by* James Parrott; *produced by* Hal Roach; *supervised by* Leo McCarey; *story by* Leo McCarey; *titles by* H.M. Walker; *photographed by* Len Powers; *edited by* Richard Currier. Filmed July 16–23 and 29–31, 1928. Running time: 20 minutes. *Cast:* Stan Laurel, Oliver Hardy, Richard Carle, Charles A. Bachman, Charley Rogers.

We Faw Down (December 29, 1928). Code: LT/BM/B3/SS/SE (silent); rating: 8. *Directed by* Leo McCarey; *produced by* Hal Roach; *titles by* H.M. Walker; *edited by* Richard Currier. Filmed August 23–September 1, 1928. Running time: 20 minutes. *Cast:* Stan Laurel, Oliver Hardy, George Kotsonaros, Bess Flowers, Vivien Oakland, Kay Deslys, Vera White, Allen Cavan.

Liberty (January 28, 1929). Code: LT/BS/SS/SE (silent); rating: 10. *Directed by* Leo McCarey; *produced by* Hal Roach; *story by* Leo McCarey; *titles by* H.M. Walker; *photographed by* George Stevens; *edited by* Richard Currier. Filmed October 1–17, 26, and November 13–19, 1928. Running time: 20 minutes. *Cast:* Stan Laurel, Oliver Hardy, James Finlayson, Tom Kennedy, Jean Harlow, Harry Bernard, Ed Brandenberg, Sam Lufkin, Jack Raymond, Jack Hill.

Wrong Again (February 28, 1929). Code: LT/B3/SS/SE (silent); rating: 8. *Directed by* Leo McCarey; *produced by* Hal Roach; *story by* Lewis R. Foster and Leo McCarey; *titles by* H.M. Walker; *photographed by* George Stevens and Jack Roach; *edited by* Richard R. Currier. Filmed November 21–December 1, 1928. Running time: 20 minutes. *Cast:* Stan Laurel, Oliver Hardy, Del Henderson, Harry Bernard, Charlie Hall, William Gillespie, Jack Hill, Sam Lufkin, Josephine Crowell, Fred Holmes.

That's My Wife (March 23, 1929). Code: LT/OM/B3/SS (silent); rating: 7. *Directed by* Lloyd French; *produced by* Hal Roach; *supervised by* Leo McCarey; *story by* Leo McCarey; *titles by* H.M. Walker; *edited by* Richard Currier. Filmed December 11–16, 1928. Running time: 20 minutes. *Cast:* Stan Laurel, Oliver Hardy, Vivien Oakland, Charlie Hall, Jimmy Aubrey, William Courtwright, Sam Lufkin, Harry Bernard.

Big Business (April 20, 1929). Code: LT/B3/SS (silent); rating: 10. *Directed by* James W. Horne; *produced by* Hal Roach; *supervised by* Leo McCarey; *story by* Leo McCarey; *titles by* H.M. Walker; *photographed by* George Stevens; *edited by* Richard Currier. Filmed December 19–26, 1928. Running time: 20 minutes. *Cast:* Stan Laurel, Oliver Hardy, James Finlayson, Stanley (Tiny) Sandford, Lyle Tayo, Retta Palmer, Charlie Hall.

Unaccustomed As We Are (May 4, 1929). Code: LS/OM/B3/SS (sound); rating: 7. *Directed by* Lewis R. Foster and Hal Roach; *produced by* Hal Roach; *story by* Leo McCarey; *dialogue by* H.M. Walker; *edited by* Richard Currier. Filmed late March–early April 1929. Running time: 20 minutes. *Cast:* Stan Laurel, Oliver Hardy, Mae Busch, Thelma Todd, Edgar Kennedy. (Note: Laurel and Hardy's first talking film, released in both sound and silent versions.)

Double Whoopee (May 18, 1929). Code: LT/SO/B3/BS/SS/SE (silent); rating: 8. *Directed by* Lewis R. Foster; *produced by* Hal Roach; *story by* Leo McCarey; *titles by* H.M. Walker; *photographed by* George Stevens and Jack Roach; *edited by* Richard Currier. Filmed February 1929. Running time: 20 minutes. *Cast:* Stan Laurel, Oliver Hardy, Jean Harlow, Charlie Hall, Ham Kinsey, Stanley (Tiny) Sandford, Rolfe Sedan, Sam Lufkin, William Gillespie, Charley Rogers, Ed Brandenberg.

Berth Marks (June 1, 1929). Code: LT/SO/SS (sound); rating: 7. *Directed by* Lewis R. Foster; *produced by* Hal Roach; *story by* Leo McCarey; *story edited by* H.M. Walker; *photographed by* Len Powers; *edited by* Richard Currier; *music by* William Axt and Yellen and Ager. Filmed April 20–27, 1929. Running time: 20 minutes. *Cast:* Stan Laurel, Oliver Hardy, Harry Bernard, Baldwin Cooke, Charlie Hall, Pat Harmon, Silas D. Wilcox.

Men o' War (June 29, 1929). Code: LT/BS/SS/SE (sound); rating: 7. *Directed by* Lewis R. Foster; *produced by* Hal Roach; *dialogue by* H.M. Walker; *photographed by* George Stevens and Jack Roach; *edited by* Richard Currier; *sound by* Elmer R. Raguse; *music by* William Axt and S. Williams. Filmed May 11–18, 1929. Running time: 20 minutes. *Cast:* Stan Laurel, Oliver Hardy, James Finlayson, Harry Bernard, Anne Cornwall, Gloria Greer, Pete Gordon, Charlie Hall, Baldwin Cooke.

Perfect Day (August 10, 1929). Code: LT/BM/SO/SS (sound); rating: 9. *Directed by* James Parrott; *produced by* Hal Roach; *story by* Hal Roach and Leo McCarey; *story edited by* H.M. Walker; *edited by* Richard Currier; *music (added in 1936) by* Marvin Hatley, Nathaniel Shilkret, and LeRoy Shield. Filmed June 8–15, 1929. Running time: 20 minutes. *Cast:* Stan Laurel, Oliver Hardy, Edgar Kennedy, Kay Deslys, Isabelle Keith, Harry Bernard, Clara Guiol, Baldwin Cooke, Lyle Tayo, Charley Rogers, Buddy (dog).

They Go Boom (September 21, 1929). Code: LT/SO/B3/SS (sound); rating: 6. *Directed by* James Parrott; *produced by* Hal Roach; *story by* Leo McCarey; *story edited by* H.M. Walker; *edited by* Richard Currier; *music by* William Axt and S. Williams. Filmed July 7–13, 1929. Running time: 20 minutes. *Cast:* Stan Laurel, Oliver Hardy, Charlie Hall, Sam Lufkin.

Bacon Grabbers (October 19, 1929). Code: LT/B3/SS (silent); rating: 7. *Directed by* Lewis R. Foster; *produced by* Hal Roach; *story by* Leo McCarey; *titles by* H.M. Walker; *photographed by* George Stevens and Jack Roach; *edited by* Richard Currier. Filmed February 16–March 2, 1929. Running time: 20 minutes. *Cast:* Stan Laurel, Oliver Hardy, Edgar Kennedy, Jean Harlow, Charlie Hall, Bobby Dunn, Eddie Baker, Sam Lufkin, Ham Kinsey (double for Laurel), Cy Slocum (double for Hardy), Buddy (dog). (Note: This film was originally released with music and sound effects on disc.)

The Hoose-Gow (November 16, 1929). Code: LT/SO/BS/SS (sound); rating: 8. *Directed by* James Parrott; *produced by* Hal Roach; *story by* Leo McCarey; *story edited by* H.M. Walker; *photographed by* George Stevens, Len Powers, and Glenn Robert Kershner; *edited by* Richard Currier; *sound by* Elmer R. Raguse; *music by* William Axt and S. Williams. Filmed August 30–September 14, 1929. Running time: 20 minutes. *Cast:* Stan Laurel, Oliver Hardy, James Finlayson, Stanley (Tiny) Sandford, Leo Willis, Dick Sutherland, Ellinor Van Der Veer, Retta Palmer, Sam Lufkin, Eddie Dunn, Baldwin Cooke, Jack Ward, Ham Kinsey, John Whiteford, Ed Brandenberg, Chet Brandenberg, Charles Dorety, Charlie Hall.

Angora Love (December 14, 1929). Code: LT/B3/SS/SE (silent); rating: 7. *Directed by* Lewis R. Foster; *produced by* Hal Roach; *story by* Leo McCarey; *titles by* H.M. Walker; *photographed by* George Stevens; *edited by* Richard Currier. Filmed March 1929. Running time: 20 minutes. *Cast:* Stan Laurel, Oliver Hardy, Edgar Kennedy, Charlie Hall, Harry Bernard, Charley Young. (Note: This film was originally released with music and sound effects on disc.)

Night Owls (January 4, 1930). Code: LT/B3/BS/SS (sound); rating: 7. *Directed by* James Parrott; *produced by* Hal Roach; *story by* Leo McCarey; *story edited by* H.M. Walker; *photographed by* George Stevens; *edited by* Richard Currier; *sound by* Elmer R. Raguse; *music by* Marvin Hatley and Harry Von Tilzer. Filmed late October–early November 1929. Running time: 20 minutes. *Cast:* Stan Laurel, Oliver Hardy, Edgar Kennedy, James Finlayson, Anders Randolph, Harry Bernard, Charles McMurphy, Baldwin Cooke.

Blotto (February 8, 1930). Code: LS/SM/B3/SS/SE (sound); rating: 8. *Directed by* James Parrott; *produced by* Hal Roach; *story by* Leo McCarey; *dialogue by* H.M. Walker; *photographed by* George Stevens; *edited by* Richard Currier; *sound by* Elmer R. Raguse; *music by* LeRoy Shield and Marvin Hatley. Filmed December 1929. Running time: 30 minutes. *Cast:* Stan Laurel, Oliver Hardy, Anita Garvin, Stanley (Tiny) Sandford, Baldwin Cooke, Charlie Hall, Frank Holliday, Dick Gilbert, Jack Hill. (Note: Spanish and French versions of this film were made for European release.)

Brats (March 22, 1930). Code: LT/BM/B3/SS/SE (sound); rating: 7. *Directed by* James Parrott; *produced by* Hal Roach; *story by* Leo McCarey and Hal Roach; *dialogue by* H.M. Walker; *photographed by*

George Stevens; *edited by* Richard Currier; *sound by* Elmer R. Raguse; *music by* Leslie-Donaldson-Skinner, Rayaf-Waller-Sisson, Mary Litt, Hackforth, Selver-Mitchell-Pollack, and Marvin Hatley. Filmed January 1930. Running time: 20 minutes. *Cast:* Stan Laurel, Oliver Hardy. (Note: German, French, and Spanish versions of this film were made for European release.)

Below Zero (April 26, 1930). Code: LT/BS/SS/SE (sound); rating: 10. *Directed by* James Parrott; *produced by* Hal Roach; *story by* Leo McCarey; *dialogue by* H.M. Walker; *photographed by* George Stevens; *edited by* Richard Currier; *sound by* Elmer R. Raguse; *music by* William Axt, Maud Nugent, Lawler, Marvin Hatley, Rayaf and Weller, and Sam Grossman. Filmed late February–early March 1930. Running time: 20 minutes. *Cast:* Stan Laurel, Oliver Hardy, Charlie Hall, Leo Willis, Stanley (Tiny) Sandford, Kay Deslys, Blanche Payson, Lyle Tayo, Retta Palmer, Baldwin Cooke, Robert Burns, Jack Hill, Charley Sullivan, Charles McMurphy, Bob O'Conor. (Note: Spanish and German versions of this film were made for European release.)

The Rogue Song (May 10, 1930). Code: LT/SO/CO/SS (sound, two-strip technicolor); rating: (film unavailable). *Directed by* Lionel Barrymore and Hal Roach; *produced by* Lionel Barrymore; *story adapted from* the 1912 opera *Gypsy Love,* by Frances Marion and John Colton; *photographed by* Percy Hilburn and C. Edgar Schoenbaum; *edited by* Margaret Booth; *art direction by* Cedric Gibbons; *sound by* Douglas Shearer and Paul Neal; *ballet music arranged by* Dmitri Tiomkin; *songs by* Herbert Stothart, Clifford Grey, and Franz Lehar. Filmed July–September 1929. Running time: 115 minutes. *Cast:* Lawrence Tibbett, Catherine Dale Owen, Judith Voselli, Nance O'Neil, Florence Lake, Lionel Belmore, Ulrich Haupt, Kate Price, Wallace McDonald, Burr McIntosh, James Bradbury, Jr., H.A. Morgan, Elsa Alsen, Stan Laurel, Oliver Hardy, Harry Bernard, The Albertina Rasch Ballet. (Note: No print of *The Rogue Song* is known to exist.)

Hog Wild (May 31, 1930). Code: LS/OM/SO/B3/SS (sound); rating: 8. *Directed by* James Parrott; *produced by* Hal Roach; *story by* Leo McCarey; *dialogue by* H.M. Walker; *photographed by* George Stevens; *edited by* Richard Currier; *sound by* Elmer R. Raguse; *music by* Hal Roach, Alice K. Howlett, Marvin Hatley, and William Axt. Filmed April 1930. Running time: 20 minutes. *Cast:* Stan Laurel, Oliver Hardy, Fay Holderness, Dorothy Granger, Charles McMurphy. (Note: French and Spanish versions of this film were made for European release.)

The Laurel-Hardy Murder Case (September 6, 1930). Code: LT/B3/SS (sound); rating: 5. *Directed by* James Parrott; *produced by* Hal Roach; *dialogue by* H.M. Walker; *photographed by* George Stevens and Walter Lundin; *edited by* Richard Currier; *sound by* Elmer R. Raguse; *music by* William Axt, Marvin Hatley, and Nathaniel Shilkret. Filmed May 1930. Running time: 30 minutes. *Cast:* Stan Laurel, Oliver Hardy, Fred Kelsey, Stanley (Tiny) Sanford, Del Henderson, Robert Burns, Dorothy Granger, Frank Austin, Lon Poff, Rosa Gore, Stanley Blystone, Art Rowlands, Ham Kinsey (double for Laurel), Cy Slocum (double for Hardy). (Note: German, Spanish, and French versions of this film were made for European release.)

Another Fine Mess (November 29, 1930). Code: LT/B3/SS/SE (sound); rating: 8. *Directed by* James Parrott; *produced by* Hal Roach; *story by* Arthur J. Jefferson (Stan Laurel's father); *dialogue by* H.M. Walker; *photographed by* George Stevens; *edited by* H.M. Walker; *sound by* Elmer R. Raguse; *music by* LeRoy Shield. Filmed late September–early October 1930. Running time: 30 minutes. *Cast:* Stan Laurel, Oliver Hardy, Thelma Todd, James Finlayson, Eddie Dunn, Charles Gerrard, Gertrude Sutton, Harry Bernard, Bill Knight, Bob Mimford, Robert Burns, Joe Mole. (Note: A Spanish version of this film was made for European release.)

Be Big (February 7, 1931). Code: LS/BM/SO/B3/SS (sound); rating: 6. *Directed by* James Parrott; *produced by* Hal Roach; *dialogue by* H.M. Walker; *photographed by* Art Lloyd; *edited by* Richard Currier; *sound by* Elmer R. Raguse; *music by* LeRoy Shield, Ring-Hager, Frederic Van Norman, Mel Kaufman, Jessie Deppen, and Marvin Hatley. Filmed late November–early December 1930. Running time: 30 minutes. *Cast:* Stan Laurel, Oliver Hardy, Anita Garvin, Isabelle Keith, Charlie Hall, Baldwin Cooke, Jack Hill, Ham Kinsey, Chet Brandenberg. (Note: French, Spanish, and German versions of this film were made for European release.)

Chickens Come Home (February 21, 1931). Code: LS/BM/B3/SS/SE (sound); rating: 7. *Directed by* James W. Horne; *produced by* Hal Roach; *dialogue by* H.M. Walker; *photographed by* Art Lloyd and Jack Stevens; *edited by* Richard Currier; *sound by* Elmer R. Raguse; *music by* LeRoy Shield, Marvin Hatley, and Alice K. Howlett. Filmed January 1931. Running time: 30 minutes. *Cast:* Stan Laurel, Oliver Hardy, Mae Busch, Thelma Todd, James Finlayson, Frank Holliday, Elizabeth Forrester, Patsy O'Byrne, Charles French, Gertrude Pedlar,

Frank Rice, Gordon Douglas, Ham Kinsey, Baldwin Cooke, Dorothy Layton. (Note: A Spanish version of this film was made for European release.)

Laughing Gravy (April 4, 1931). Code: LT/B3/SS/SE (sound); rating: 8. *Directed by* James W. Horne; *produced by* Hal Roach; *dialogue by* H.M. Walker; *photographed by* Art Lloyd; *edited by* Richard Currier; *music by* LeRoy Shield and Marvin Hatley. Filmed February 1931. Running time: 20 minutes. *Cast:* Stan Laurel, Oliver Hardy, Charlie Hall, Harry Bernard, Charles Dorety, Laughing Gravy (dog). (Note: French, Spanish, and German versions of this film, all with additional footage and incorporating *Be Big,* were made for European release.)

Our Wife (May 16, 1931). Code: LT/SO/B3/SS/SE (sound); rating: 9. *Directed by* James W. Horne; *produced by* Hal Roach; *dialogue by* H.M. Walker; *photographed by* Art Lloyd; *edited by* Richard Currier; *sound by* Elmer R. Raguse; *music by* LeRoy Shield and Marvin Hatley. Filmed March 1931. Running time: 20 minutes. *Cast:* Stan Laurel, Oliver Hardy, Jean London, James Finlayson, Ben Turpin, Charley Rogers, Blanche Payson.

Pardon Us (August 15, 1931). Code: LT/BS/SS (sound); rating: 6. *Directed by* James Parrott; *produced by* Hal Roach; *dialogue by* H.M. Walker; *photographed by* George Stevens; *edited by* Richard Currier; *sound by* Elmer R. Raguse; *music by* LeRoy Shield, Edward Kilenyi, Arthur J. Lamb, H.W. Petrie, Will Marion Cook, Irving Berlin, Cole and Johnston, Abe Olman, M. Ewing, Frederic Van Norman, L.E. deFrancesco, J.S. Jamecnik, Freita Shaw, and Marvin Hatley. Filmed August–December 1930. Running time: 56 minutes. *Cast:* Stan Laurel, Oliver Hardy, Walter Long, James Finlayson, June Marlowe, Charlie Hall, Wilfred Lucas, Frank Holliday, Harry Bernard, Stanley (Tiny) Sandford, Robert Burns, Frank Austin, Otto Fries, Robert Kortman, Leo Willis, Jerry Mandy, Bobby Dunn, Eddie Dunn, Baldwin Cooke, Charles Dorety, Dick Gilbert, Will Stanton, Jack Herrick, Jack Hill, Gene Morgan, Charles A. Bachman, John Whiteford, Charley Rogers, Gordon Douglas, James Parrott, Hal Roach, Eddie Baker, and the Etude Ethiopian Chorus. (Note: French, German, and Spanish versions of this film were made for European release.)

Come Clean (September 19, 1931). Code: LS/BM/B3/SS/SE (sound); rating: 9. *Directed by* James W. Horne; *produced by* Hal

Roach; *dialogue by* H.M. Walker; *photographed by* Art Lloyd; *edited by* Richard Currier; *sound by* Elmer R. Raguse; *music by* LeRoy Shield, John Philip Sousa, and Marvin Hatley. Filmed May 1931. Running time: 20 minutes. *Cast:* Stan Laurel, Oliver Hardy, Gertrude Astor, Linda Loredo, Mae Busch, Charlie Hall, Eddie Baker, Stanley (Tiny) Sandford, Gordon Douglas.

One Good Turn (October 31, 1931). Code: LT/SO/BS/SS/SE (sound); rating: 8. *Directed by* James W. Horne; *produced by* Hal Roach; *dialogue by* H.M. Walker; *photographed by* Art Lloyd; *edited by* Richard Currier; *sound by* Elmer R. Raguse; *music by* LeRoy Shield and Marvin Hatley. Filmed June 1931. Running time: 20 minutes. *Cast:* Stan Laurel, Oliver Hardy, Mary Carr, James Finlayson, Billy Gilbert, Lyle Tayo, Dorothy Granger, Snub Pollard, Gordon Douglas, Dick Gilbert, George Miller, Baldwin Cooke, Ham Kinsey, Retta Palmer, William Gillespie, Charley Young.

Beau Hunks (December 12, 1931). Code: LT/BS/SS/SE (sound); rating: 7. *Directed by* James W. Horne; *produced by* Hal Roach; *dialogue by* H.M. Walker; *photographed by* Art Lloyd and Jack Stevens; *edited by* Richard Currier; *sound by* Elmer R. Raguse; *music by* LeRoy Shield, Herbert Ingraham, Riesenfeld, and Marvin Hatley. Filmed September 1931. Running time: 40 minutes. *Cast:* Stan Laurel, Oliver Hardy, Charles Middleton, Charlie Hall, Stanley (Tiny) Sandford, Harry Schultz, Gordon Douglas, Sam Lufkin, Marvin Hatley, Jack Hill, Leo Willis, Bob Kortman, Baldwin Cooke, Dick Gilbert, Oscar Morgan, Ham Kinsey, Broderick O'Farrell, James W. Horne, Jean Harlow (in photograph only). (Note: French and Spanish versions of this film were made for European release.)

Helpmates (January 23, 1932). Code: LS/OM/SO/SS/SE (sound); rating: 10. *Directed by* James Parrott; *produced by* Hal Roach; *dialogue by* H.M. Walker; *photographed by* Art Lloyd; *edited by* Richard Currier; *music by* Leroy Shield and Marvin Hatley. Filmed late October 1931. Running time: 20 minutes. *Cast:* Stan Laurel, Oliver Hardy, Blanche Payson, Robert Burns, Robert Callahan.

Any Old Port (March 5, 1932). Code: LT/B3/SS (sound); rating: 6. *Directed by* James W. Horne; *produced by* Hal Roach; *dialogue by* H.M. Walker; *photographed by* Art Lloyd; *edited by* Richard Currier; *sound by* Elmer R. Raguse; *music by* LeRoy Shield and Marvin Hatley. Filmed late November 1931. Running time: 20 minutes. *Cast:* Stan

Laurel, Oliver Hardy, Walter Long, Jacqueline Wells/Julie Bishop, Harry Bernard, Charlie Hall, Robert Burns, Sam Lufkin, Dick Gilbert, Eddie Baker, Will Stanton, Jack Hill, Baldwin Cooke, Ed Brandenberg.

The Music Box (April 16, 1932). Code: LT/B3/SS/SE (sound); rating: 10. *Directed by* James Parrott; *produced by* Hal Roach; *dialogue by* H.M. Walker; *photographed by* Walter Lundin and Len Powers; *edited by* Richard Currier; *sound by* James Greene; *music by* LeRoy Shield, Francis Scott Key, Marvin Hatley, and Harry Graham. Filmed December 1931. Running time: 30 minutes. *Cast:* Stan Laurel, Oliver Hardy, Billy Gilbert, William Gillespie, Charlie Hall, Gladys Gale, Sam Lufkin, Lilyan Irene, Marvin Hatley (playing piano, off-camera), Susie (horse). (Note: This film won an Academy Award for "Best Live-Action Comedy Short of 1931-32.")

The Chimp (May 21, 1932). Code: LT/B3/SS/SE (sound); rating: 7. *Directed by* James Parrott; *produced by* Hal Roach; *dialogue by* H.M. Walker; *photographed by* Walter Lundin; *edited by* Richard Currier; *sound by* Elmer R. Raguse; *music by* LeRoy Shield, Walt Eufel, Marvin Matley, Rosas, John Philip Sousa, and John N. Klohr. Filmed late January–early February 1932. Running time: 30 minutes. *Cast:* Stan Laurel, Oliver Hardy, Billy Gilbert, James Finlayson, Stanley (Tiny) Sandford, Charles Gamora, Jack Hill, Robert Burns, George Miller, Baldwin Cooke, Dorothy Layton, Belle Hare, Martha Sleeper.

County Hospital (June 25, 1932). Code: LS/SO/SS/SE (sound); rating: 7. *Directed by* James Parrott; *produced by* Hal Roach; *dialogue by* H.M. Walker; *photographed by* Art Lloyd; *edited by* Richard Currier; *sound by* James Greene; *music by* LeRoy Shield and Marvin Hatley. Filmed late February 1932. Running time: 20 minutes. *Cast:* Stan Laurel, Oliver Hardy, Billy Gilbert, Sam Lufkin, Baldwin Cooke, Ham Kinsey, May Wallace, Frank Holliday, Lilyan Irene, Belle Hare, Dorothy Layton, William Austin.

Scram (September 10, 1932). Code: LT/B3/BS/SS/SE (sound); rating: 8. *Directed by* Raymond McCarey; *produced by* Hal Roach; *dialogue by* H.M. Walker; *photographed by* Art Lloyd; *edited by* Richard Currier; *sound by* James Greene; *music by* LeRoy Shield, Marvin Hatley, Ring-Hager, Warren-Green, and J.S. Zamecnik. Filmed June 18–July 1, 1932. Running time: 20 minutes. *Cast:* Stan Laurel, Oliver Hardy, Arthur Housman, Rychard Cramer, Vivien Oakland, Sam Lufkin, Charles McMurphy, Baldwin Cooke, Charles Dorety.

Pack Up Your Troubles (September 17, 1932). Code: LT/BS/SS/SE (sound); rating: 8. *Directed by* George Marshall; *produced by* Hal Roach; *dialogue by* H.M. Walker; *photographed by* Art Lloyd; *edited by* Richard Currier; *sound by* James Greene; *music by* LeRoy Shield and Marvin Hatley. Filmed early May–early June 1932. Running time: 68 minutes. *Cast:* Stan Laurel, Oliver Hardy, Tom Kennedy, Grady Sutton, Donald Dillaway, Jacquie Lyn, Mary Carr, Billy Gilbert, C. Montague Shaw, Muriel Evans, James Finlayson, Al Hallet, Bill O'Brien, Mary Gordon, Lew Kelly, Frank Brownlee, George Marshall, Charley Rogers, Frank Rice, Charles Dorety, Charles Middleton, Nora Cecil, Jack Hill, Ham Kinsey, Dorothy Layton, Marvin Hatley, Ben Hendricks, Jr., Pat Harmon, Bud Fine, Frank S. Hagney, Bob O'Conor, Pete Gordon, Baldwin Cooke, Henry Hall, Ellinor Van Der Veer, Charlie Hall, Robert Emmett Homans, George Miller, Chet Brandenberg, Richard Tucker, Rychard Cramer.

Their First Mistake (November 5, 1932). Code: LT/OM/B3/SS/SE (sound); rating: 9. *Directed by* George Marshall; *produced by* Hal Roach; *edited by* Richard Currier; *sound by* James Greene; *music by* Marvin Hatley and LeRoy Shield. Filmed September 24–October 1, 1932. Running time: 20 minutes. *Cast:* Stan Laurel, Oliver Hardy, Mae Busch, Billy Gilbert, George Marshall.

Towed in a Hole (December 31, 1932). Code: LT/SO/SS/SE (sound); rating: 10. *Directed by* George Marshall; *produced by* Hal Roach; *story by* Stan Laurel; *photographed by* Art Lloyd; *edited by* Richard Currier; *sound by* James Greene; *music by* LeRoy Shield and Marvin Hatley. Filmed November 1–10, 1932. Running time: 20 minutes. *Cast:* Stan Laurel, Oliver Hardy, Billy Gilbert.

Twice Two (February 25, 1933). Code: LS/BM/SO/SS (sound); rating: 4. *Directed by* James Parrott; *produced by* Hal Roach; *photographed by* Art Lloyd; *edited by* Bert Jordan; *sound by* James Greene; *music by* Marvin Hatley and LeRoy Shield. Filmed late November 1932. Running time: 20 minutes. *Cast:* Stan Laurel, Oliver Hardy, Baldwin Cooke, Charlie Hall, Ham Kinsey, Carol Tevis (voice-over for Mrs. Hardy), Mae Wallace (voice-over for Mrs. Laurel).

Me and My Pal (April 22, 1933). Code: LS/SO/SS/SE (sound); rating: 8. *Directed by* Charles Rogers; *produced by* Hal Roach; *photographed by* Art Lloyd; *edited by* Bert Jordan; *sound by* James Greene; *music by* LeRoy Shield, Wagner, and Marvin Hatley. Filmed March 1933.

Running time: 20 minutes. *Cast:* Stan Laurel, Oliver Hardy, James Finlayson, James C. Morton, Eddie Dunn, Charlie Hall, Bobby Dunn, Carroll Borland, Mary Kornman, Charles McMurphy, Eddie Baker, Marion Bardell, Charley Young, Walter Plinge.

The Devil's Brother (May 5, 1933). (Also known as *Fra Diavolo*.) Code: LT/B3/CO/SS/SE (sound); rating: 9. *Directed by* Hal Roach and Charles Rogers; *produced by* Hal Roach; *story adapted from* Daniel F. Auber's 1830 opera, *Fra Diavolo*, by Jeanie MacPherson; *photographed by* Art Lloyd and Hap Depew; *edited by* Bert Jordan and William Terhune; *sound by* James Greene; *music by* Auber; *musical direction by* LeRoy Shield. Filmed February 4–March 4, 1933. Running time: 90 minutes. *Cast:* Stan Laurel, Oliver Hardy, Dennis King, Thelma Todd, James Finlayson, Henry Armetta, Lane Chandler, Arthur Pierson, Lucille Browne, George Miller, Stanley (Tiny) Sandford, James C. Morton, Nina Quartaro, Jack Hill, Dick Gilbert, Arthur Stone, John Qualen, Edith Fellows, Jackie Taylor, Rolfe Sedan, Kay Deslys, Leo Willis, Lillian Moore, Walter Shumway, Louise Carver, Matt McHugh, Harry Bernard, Wilfred Lucas, Carl Harbaugh.

The Midnight Patrol (August 3, 1933). Code: LT/SO/B3/SS/SE (sound); rating: 7. *Directed by* Lloyd French; *produced by* Hal Roach; *photographed by* Art Lloyd; *edited by* Bert Jordan; *sound by* James Greene; *music by* Marvin Hatley and LeRoy Shield. Filmed June 24–July 6, 1933. Running time: 20 minutes. *Cast:* Stan Laurel, Oliver Hardy, Robert Kortman, Charlie Hall, Walter Plinge, Harry Bernard, Frank Brownlee, James C. Morton, Stanley (Tiny) Sandford, Edgar Dearing, Eddie Dunn, Billy Bletcher.

Busy Bodies (October 7, 1933). Code: LT/SO/B3/SS (sound); rating: 9. *Directed by* Lloyd French; *produced by* Hal Roach; *photographed by* Art Lloyd; *edited by* Bert Jordan; *sound by* James Greene; *music by* LeRoy Shield, Marvin Hatley, and Alice K. Howlett. Filmed July 15–25, 1933. Running time: 20 minutes. *Cast:* Stan Laurel, Oliver Hardy, Stanley (Tiny) Sandford, Charlie Hall, Jack Hill, Dick Gilbert, Charley Young.

Dirty Work (November 25, 1933). Code: LT/SO/B3/SS (sound); rating: 8. *Directed by* Lloyd French; *produced by* Hal Roach; *photographed by* Kenneth Peach; *edited by* Bert Jordan; *sound by* William B. Delaplain; *music by* Marvin Hatley and LeRoy Shield. Filmed

August 7–19, 1933. Running time: 20 minutes. *Cast:* Stan Laurel, Oliver Hardy, Lucien Littlefield, Sam Adams, Jiggs (chimpanzee).

Sons of the Desert (December 29, 1933). Code: LS/BM/B3/SS/SE (sound); rating: 10. *Directed by* William A. Seiter and Lloyd French; *produced by* Hal Roach; *story by* Frank Craven; *continuity by* Byron Morgan; *photographed by* Kenneth Peach; *edited by* Bert Jordan; *sound by* Harry Baker; *music by* Marvin Hatley, William Axt, George M. Cohan, O'Donnell-Heath, Marquardt, and LeRoy Shield. Filmed October 2–23, 1933. Running time: 68 minutes. *Cast:* Stan Laurel, Oliver Hardy, Charley Chase, Mae Busch, Dorothy Christie, Lucien Littlefield, John Elliot, Charley Young, John Merton, William Gillespie, Charles McAvoy, Robert Burns, Al Thompson, Eddie Baker, Jimmy Aubrey, Chet Brandenberg, Don Brodie, Philo McCullough, Charita, Harry Bernard, Sam Lufkin, Ernie Alexander, Charlie Hall, Baldwin Cooke, Stanley Blystone, Max Wagner, Pat Harmon, Ty Parvis, Bob Cummings, Billy Gilbert, The Hollywood American Legion Post, The Santa Monica Lodge of Elks.

Oliver the Eighth (January 13, 1934). Code: LT/B3/SS/SE (sound); rating: 7. *Directed by* Lloyd French; *produced by* Hal Roach; *photographed by* Art Lloyd; *edited by* Bert Jordan; *sound by* William B. Delaplain; *music by* LeRoy Shield and Ray Henderson. Filmed December 15–20, 1933, and mid–January 1934. Running time: 30 minutes. *Cast:* Stan Laurel, Oliver Hardy, Mae Busch, Jack Barty.

Going Bye-Bye! (June 23, 1934). Code: LT/B3/SS (sound); rating: 8. *Directed by* Charles Rogers; *produced by* Hal Roach; *photographed by* Francis Corby; *edited by* Bert Jordan; *sound by* Harry Baker; *music by* LeRoy Shield. Filmed May 21–26, 1934. Running time: 20 minutes. *Cast:* Stan Laurel, Oliver Hardy, Walter Long, Mae Busch, Sam Lufkin, Harry Dunkinson, Ellinor Van Der Veer, Baldwin Cooke, Fred Holmes, Jack Lipson, Lester Dorr, Charles Dorety.

Them Thar Hills (July 21, 1934). Code: LT/B3/SS/SE (sound); rating: 8. *Directed by* Charles Rogers; *produced by* Hal Roach; *photographed by* Art Lloyd; *edited by* Bert Jordan; *sound by* James Greene; *music by* LeRoy Shield, Marvin Hatley, and Hill. Filmed June 11–20, 1934. Running time: 20 minutes. *Cast:* Stan Laurel, Oliver Hardy, Billy Gilbert, Charlie Hall, Mae Busch, Bobby Dunn, Sam Lufkin, Dick Alexander, Eddie Baker, Baldwin Cooke, Robert Burns.

Babes in Toyland (November 30, 1934). Code: LT/B3/CO/SS/SE (sound); rating: 9. *Directed by* Charles Rogers and Gus Meins; *produced by* Hal Roach; *screenplay by* Nick Grinde and Frank Butler; *adapted from the operetta by* Victor Herbert and the book by Glen Mac-Donough; *photographed by* Art Lloyd and Francis Corby; *edited by* William Terhune and Bert Jordan; *sound by* Elmer R. Raguse; *music by* Victor Herbert, Glen MacDonough, Ann Ronell, and Frank Churchill; *musical direction by* Harry Jackson. Filmed August 6–16 and September 24–October 17, 1934. Running time: 79 minutes. *Cast:* Stan Laurel, Oliver Hardy, Charlotte Henry, Felix Knight, Harry Kleinbach/Henry Brandon, Johnny Downs, Jean Darling, Marie Wilson, Virginia Karns, Florence Roberts, William Burress, Ferdinand Munier, Frank Austin, Gus Leonard, John George, Scotty Beckett, Marianne Edwards, Tommy Bupp, Georgie Billings, Jerry Tucker, Jackie Taylor, Dickie Jones, Alice Dahl, Pete Gordon, Sumner Getchell, Billy Bletcher, Payne Johnson, Angelo Rossito, Charley Rogers, Alice Moore, Alice Cooke, Kewpie Morgan, Stanley (Tiny) Sandford, Eddie Baker, Dick Alexander, Richard Powell, Scott Mattraw, Fred Holmes, Jack Raymond, Eddie Borden, Sam Lufkin, Jack Hill, Baldwin Cooke, Charlie Hall.

The Live Ghost (December 8, 1934). Code: LT/B3/SS (sound); rating: 7. *Directed by* Charles Rogers; *produced by* Hal Roach; *dialogue by* H.M. Walker; *photographed by* Art Lloyd; *edited by* Louis Mac-Manus; *sound by* Elmer Raguse; *music by* Marvin Hatley, Irving Berlin, Arthur Kay, and LeRoy Shield. Filmed November 8–14, 1934. Running time: 20 minutes. *Cast:* Stan Laurel, Oliver Hardy, Walter Long, Mae Busch, Arthur Housman, Harry Bernard, Pete Gordon, Leo Willis, Charlie Hall, Charlie Sullivan, Jack Lipson, Sam Lufkin, Dick Gilbert, Baldwin Cooke, Arthur Rowlands, Hubert Diltz, Bill Moore, John Power.

Tit for Tat (January 5, 1935). Code: LT/B3/SS/SE (sound); rating: 8. *Directed by* Charles Rogers; *produced by* Hal Roach; *photographed by* Art Lloyd; *edited by* Bert Jordan; *sound by* William Randall; *music by* LeRoy Shield and Marvin Hatley. Filmed December 10–20, 1934. Running time: 20 minutes. *Cast:* Stan Laurel, Oliver Hardy, Charlie Hall, Mae Busch, James C. Morton, Bobby Dunn, Baldwin Cooke, Jack Hill, Pete Gordon, Elsie MacKaye, Dick Gilbert, Lester Dorr, Viola Richard. (Note: This film is the only Laurel and Hardy sequel, a continuation of *Them Thar Hills,* 1934.)

The Fixer-Uppers (February 9, 1935). Code: LT/B3/SS/SE (sound); rating: 8. *Directed by* Charles Rogers; *produced by* Hal Roach;

photographed by Art Lloyd; *edited by* Bert Jordan; *sound by* James Greene; *music by* LeRoy Shield and Marvin Hatley. Filmed January 11–19, 1935. Running time: 20 minutes. *Cast:* Stan Laurel, Oliver Hardy, Mae Busch, Charles Middleton, Arthur Housman, Bobby Dunn, Noah Young, Dick Gilbert, Jack Hill, James C. Morton, Bob O'Conor.

Thicker Than Water (August 6, 1935). Code LT/OM/B3/SS/SE (sound); rating: 9. *Directed by* James W. Horne; *produced by* Hal Roach; *story by* Stan Laurel; *photographed by* Art Lloyd; *edited by* Ray Snyder; *music by* LeRoy Shield and Marvin Hatley. Filmed July 1–8, 1935. Running time: 20 minutes. *Cast:* Stan Laurel, Oliver Hardy, Daphne Pollard, James Finlayson, Harry Bowen, Ed Brandenberg, Charlie Hall, Grace Goodall, Bess Flowers, Lester Dorr, Gladys Gale, Allen Cavan, Baldwin Cooke.

Bonnie Scotland (August 23, 1935). Code: LT/B3/BS/SS/SE (sound); rating: 8. *Directed by* James W. Horne; *produced by* Hal Roach; *screenplay by* Frank Butler and Jefferson Moffitt; *photographed by* Art Lloyd and Walter Lundin; *edited by* Bert Jordan; *sound by* Elmer R. Raguse; *music by* LeRoy Shield and Marvin Hatley. Filmed May 1–June 15, 1935. Running time: 80 minutes. *Cast:* Stan Laurel, Oliver Hardy, Anne Grey, David Torrnece, June Vlasek/June Lang, William Janney, James Mack, James Finlayson, Mary Gordon, May Beatty, Daphne Pollard, James May, Jack Hill, Kathryn Sheldon, Minerva Urecal, Margaret Mann, Claire Verdera, Maurice Black, Vernon Steele, Noah Young, Dan Maxwell, David Clyde, James Burtis, Brandon Hurst, Olaf Hytten, Marvin Hatley, Claude King, Bill Moore, Art Rowlands, Frank Benson, Gunnis Davis, Lionel Belmore, Dick Wessell, Charlie Hall, Bob O'Conor, Leo Willis, Sam Lufkin, Bobby Dunn, Carlos J. deValdez, Lal Chand Mehra, Anthony Francis, Raizada Devinder Nath Bali, Phyllis Barry, Belle Daube, Elizabeth Wilbur, Colin Kenny, Pat Somerset, Jack Deery, Colonel McDonnell, Clive Morgan, Major Harris, Jay Belasco, Carlotta Monti, Hona Hoy, Vaino Hassan, Julia Halia, Shura Shermet, Gurdial Singh, Eddie Dass, Bogwhan Singh, Otto Frisco, Abdullah Hassan, Ted Oliver, Murdock Mac-Quarrie, John Power, Barlowe Borland, Frances Morris, Mary McLaren, John Sutherland's Scotch Pipers.

The Bohemian Girl (February 14, 1936). Code: LT/OM/BS/CO/SS/SE (sound); rating: 7. *Directed by* James W. Horne and Charles Rogers; *produced by* Hal Roach; *supervised by* L.A. French; *story adapted from* Michael W. Balfe's 1843 opera; *photographed by* Art Lloyd and Francis Corby; *edited by* Bert Jordan and Louis MacManus; *art direction by* Arthur I. Royce and William L. Stevens; *sound by* Elmer R. Raguse; *music by* Balfe, Nathaniel Shilkret, and Robert Shayon; *musical direction by* Nathaniel Shilkret. Filmed October 9–November 30, 1935. Running time: 70 minutes. *Cast:* Stan Laurel, Oliver Hardy, Thelma Todd, Jacqueline Wells/Julie Bishop, Darla Hood, James Finlayson, Mae Busch, Antonia Moreno, Harry Bowen, Zeffie Tilbury, William P. Carlton, Harry Bernard, Mitchell Lewis, Andrea Leeds, Margaret Mann, Harold Switzer, James C. Morton, Eddie Borden, Sam Lufkin, Bob O'Conor, Bobby Dunn, Felix Knight, Dick Gilbert, Leo Willis, Jack Hill, Arthur Rowlands, Lane Chandler, Baldwin Cooke, Lee Phelps, Bill Madsen, Frank Darien, Sammy Brooks, Howard Hickman, Edward Erle, Alice Cooke, Tony Campenero, Jerry Breslin, Eddy Chandler, Rita Dunn, Charlie Hall, Yogi (myna bird), Laughing Gravy (dog).

Our Relations (October 30, 1936). Code: LT/BM/B3/SS/SE (sound); rating: 10. *Directed by* Harry Lachman; *produced by* Stan Laurel; *supervised by* L.A. French; *adapted from* the W.W. Jacobs story, "The Money Box," by Charles Rogers and Jack Jevne; *screenplay by* Richard Connell and Felix Adler; *photographed by* Rudolph Maté; *photographic effects by* Roy Seawright; *edited by* Bert Jordan; *art direction by* Arthur I. Royce and William L. Stevens; *music by* LeRoy Shield. Filmed March 16–May 4, 1936. Running time: 74 minutes. *Cast:* Stan Laurel, Oliver Hardy, Sidney Toler, Alan Hale, Daphne Pollard, Betty Healy, Iris Adrian, Lona Andre, James Finlayson, Arthur Housman, Jim Kilganon, Charlie Hall, Harry Bernard, Harry Arras, Charles A. Bachman, Harry Neilman, John Kelly, Art Rowlands, Harry Wilson, Baldwin Cooke, Nick Copland, James C. Morton, Lee Phelps, George Jimenez, Bob Wilbur, Jim Pierce, Ruth Warren, Walter Taylor, Constantine Romanoff, Alex Pollard, Joe Bordeaux, Stanley (Tiny) Sandford, Billy Engle, Bob O'Conor, Bobby Dunn, Ralf Harolde, Noel Madison, Del Henderson, Fred Holmes, Bob Finlayson, Alex Finlayson, Foxy Hall, Jay Eaton, Jack Hill, Rita Dunn, Alice Cooke, Ed Brandenberg, Jack Egan, Bunny Bronson, Marvel Andre, Dick Gilbert, Jack Cooper, Jerry Breslin, Bill Madsen, Ernie Alexander, Tony Campenero, Polly Chase, Jay Belasco, Gertrude Astor, Buddy Messinger, Gertie Messenger Sharpe, David Sharpe, Rose Langdon, Johnny Arthur, Kay McCoy, Mrs. Jack W. Burns, Rheba Campbell, Margo Sage, Ed Parker, Leo Sulkey, Marvin Hatley, Sam Lufkin, Barney O'Toole, Ray Cooke, Art Miles, Crete Sipple, Dick French, Rosemary Theby.

Way Out West (April 16, 1937). Code: LT/B3/SS/SE (sound); rating: 10. *Directed by* James W. Horne; *produced by* Stan Laurel; *story by* Jack Jevne and Charles Rogers; *screenplay by* Charles Rogers, Felix Adler, and James Parrott; *photographed by* Art Lloyd and Walter Lundin; *photographic effects by* Roy Seawright; *edited by* Bert Jordan; *art direction by* Arthur I. Royce; *sound by* William Randall; *music by* Marvin Hatley. Filmed August 27–early November 1936. Running time: 65 minutes. *Cast:* Stan Laurel, Oliver Hardy, James Finlayson, Sharon Lynne, Stanley Fields, Rosina Lawrence, James Mason, James C. Morton, Frank Mills, Dave Pepper, Vivien Oakland, Harry Bernard, Mary Gordon, May Wallace, Chill Wills, Art Green, Walter Trask, Don Brookins, Jack Hill, Sam Lufkin, Tex Driscoll, Flora Flinch, Fred Toones, Bobby Dunn, John Ince, Fritzi Brunette, Frank Montgomery, Bill Wolf, Denver Dixon/Art Mix, Fred Cady, Eddie Borden, Helen Holmes, Ben Corbett, Buffalo Bill, Jr., Jay Wilsey, Cy Slocum (character and double for Hardy), Lester Dorr, Ham Kinsey (double for Laurel), Dinah (mule). (Note: This film received an Academy Award nomination for "Best Original Music Score for 1936–37.")

Swiss Miss (May 20, 1938). Code: LT/B3/CO/SS/SE (sound); rating: 7. *Directed by* John G. Blystone and Hal Roach; *produced by* Hal Roach; *story by* Jean Negulesco, Charles Rogers, Stan Laurel, and Hal Roach; *screenplay by* James Parrott, Felix Adler, and Charles Melson; *photographed by* Norbert Brodine and Art Lloyd; *photographic effects by* Roy Seawright; edited by Bert Jordan; *art direction by* Charles D. Hall; *set decorations by* William L. Stevens; *sound by* William Randall; *music by* LeRoy Shield, Phil Charig, Arthur Quenzer, Nathaniel Shilkret, Freedman-Slater, and Marvin Hatley; *musical arrangements by* Arthur Morton; *musical direction by* Marvin Hatley. Filmed December 28, 1937–February 26, 1938. Running time: 72 minutes. *Cast:* Stan Laurel, Oliver Hardy, Walter Woolf King, Della Lind/Grete Batzler, Adia Kuznetzoff, Eddie Kane, Anita Garvin, Franz Hug, Eric Blore, Ludovico Tomarchio, Sam Lufkin, Tex Driscoll, Charles Judels, George Sorel, Harry Semels, Etherine Landucci, Gustav von Seyffertitz, Conrad Seideman, Joseph Struder, Louis Struder, Otto Jehle, Fritz Wolfesberger, Bob O'Conor, Michael Mark, Jean de Briac, Agostino Borgato, Jacques Vanaire, James Carson, Ed Searpa, Winstead Weaver, Hal Gerard, Nick Copeland, George Granlich, Earl Douglas, Alex Melesh, Jack Lubell, Eddie Brain, Eddie Johnson, Baldwin Cooke, Ed Brandenberg, Jack Hill, Lester Dorr, Val Raset, Ham Kinsey (double for Laurel), Cy Slocum (double for Hardy), Charles Gamora, Dinah (mule).

Block-Heads (August 19, 1938). Code: LS/OM/B3/SS/SE (sound); rating: 9. *Directed by* John G. Blystone; *produced by* Hal Roach; *associate production by* Hal Roach, Jr.; *supervised by* Sidney S. Van Keuran; *story and screenplay by* Charles Rogers, Felix Adler, James Parrott, Harry Langdon, and Arnold Belgard; *photographed by* Art Lloyd; *photographic effects by* Roy Seawright; *edited by* Bert Jordan; *sound by* Hal Bumbaugh; *music by* Marvin Hatley. Filmed June 1–July 1 and July 27–28, 1938. Running time: 58 minutes. *Cast:* Stan Laurel, Oliver Hardy, Billy Gilbert, Patricia Ellis, Minna Gombell, James C. Morton, James Finlayson, Harry Woods, Tommy Bond, Jean del Val, Henry Hall, Sam Lufkin, Harry Strang, William Royle, Harry Earles, Max Hoffman, Jr., Patsy Moran, Ed Brandenberg, Jack Hill, George Chandler, Harry Stubbs, Ham Kinsey (double for Laurel), Cy Slocum (double for Hardy). (Note: This film received an Academy Award nomination for "Best Original Music Score for 1937–38.")

A Chump at Oxford (February 16, 1940). Code: LT/SO/B3/SS/SE (sound); rating: 8. *Directed by* Alfred Goulding; *produced by* Hal Roach; *associate production by* Hal Roach, Jr.; *story and screenplay by* Charles Rogers, Felix Adler, and Harry Langdon; *photographed by* Art Lloyd; *photographic effects by* Roy Seawright; *edited by* Bert Jordan; *art direction by* Charles D. Hall; *set decorations by* William L. Stevens; *sound by* William Randall; *music by* Marvin Hatley. Filmed June and September 1939. Running time: 63 minutes. *Cast:* Stan Laurel, Oliver Hardy, Forrester Harvey, Wilfred Lucas, Forbes Murray, Frank Baker, Eddie Borden, Peter Cushing, Charlie Hall, Gerald Fielding, Victor Kendall, Gerald Rogers, Jack Heasley, Rex Lease, Stanley Blystone, Alec Hartford, James Finlayson, Anita Garvin, Vivien Oakland, James Millican, Harry Bernard, Sam Lufkin, Jean de Briac, George Magrill.

Saps at Sea (May 3, 1940). Code: LT/B3/SS/SE (sound); rating: 8. *Directed by* Gordon Douglas; *produced by* Hal Roach; *supervised by* Sidney S. Van Keuran; *story and screenplay by* Charles Rogers, Felix Adler, Gil Pratt, and Harry Langdon; *photographed by* Art Lloyd; *photographic effects by* Roy Seawright; *edited by* William Ziegler; *art direction by* Charles D. Hall; *set decorations by* William L. Stevens; *sound by* Elmer R. Raguse and William B. Delaplain; *music by* Marvin Hatley and LeRoy Shield. Filmed November–early December 1939. Running time: 57 minutes. *Cast:* Stan Laurel, Oliver Hardy, James Finlayson, Ben Turpin, Rychard Cramer, Eddie Conrad, Harry Hayden, Charlie Hall, Patsy Morgan, Gene Morgan, Charles A. Bachman, Bud Geary, Jack Greene, Eddie Borden, Robert McKenzie, Ernie Alexander,

Mary Gordon, Jack Hill, Walter Lawrence, Carl Faulkner, Harry
Evans, Ed Brady, Patsy O'Byrne, Francesca Santaro, Jackie Horner,
Harry Bernard, Sam Lufkin, Constantine Romanoff, Narcissus (goat).

*Following is a listing of personnel for the only film Laurel and
Hardy appeared in before being teamed at Roach Studios in 1926. Appearing together completely by accident, Stan is the star, while Ollie has
a one-minute bit part.*

The Lucky Dog (1919). Rating: 3 (silent). *Directed by* Jess Robbins;
produced by G.M. (Broncho Billy) Anderson; *released by* Sunkist Pictures. Filmed November 17–29, 1919. Running time: 20 minutes. *Cast:*
Stan Laurel, Florence Gillet, Oliver Hardy.

*Laurel and Hardy also made cameo appearances in other major
films while under contract to Hal Roach Studios. Following is a list of
these motion pictures.*

The Hollywood Revue of 1929 (November 23, 1929), sound. *Directed by* Charles F. Riesner, Lionel Barrymore, Jack Cummings, Sandy
Roth, and Al Shenberg; *produced by* Harry Rapf; *released by* Metro-
Goldwyn-Mayer Pictures. Filmed Spring 1929. Running time: 120 minutes. (Laurel and Hardy appear as magicians in two brief sequences of
this film, which also features Jack Benny, Conrad Nagel, Joan
Crawford, Buster Keaton, and Lionel Barrymore.)

The Stolen Jools (April 1931), sound. *Directed by* William McGann;
produced by Pat Casey; *supervised by* E.K. Nadel; *released by* Para-
mount Pictures. Filmed early 1931. Running time: 20 minutes. (Laurel
and Hardy appear for less than a minute, in a scene in which their
auto falls apart, in this "all-star" short. Also featured are Wallace
Beery, Buster Keaton, Joan Crawford, Edward G. Robinson, and Gary
Cooper.)

On the Loose (December 26, 1931), sound. *Directed by* Hal Roach;
produced by Hal Roach; *story by* Hal Roach; *dialogue by* H.M. Walker;
photographed by Len Powers; *edited by* Richard Currier; *released by*
Metro-Goldwyn-Mayer Pictures. Filmed September 1931. Running time:
20 minutes. (In this Thelma Todd–Zazu Pitts short, Laurel and Hardy
appear in the final scene, asking the two women for dates.)

Wild Poses (October 28, 1933), sound. *Directed by* Robert F. McGowan; *produced by* Robert F. McGowan (for Hal Roach); *photographed by* Francis Corby; *edited by* William Terhune; *released by* Metro-Goldwyn-Mayer Pictures. Filmed August 1933. Running time: 20 minutes. (In this Our Gang short, Laurel and Hardy appear as babies for a total of 20 seconds of screen time.)

Hollywood Party (June 1, 1934), sound. *Directed by* Richard Boleslawski, Allan Dwan, and Roy Rowland; *produced by* Harry Rapf and Howard Dietz; *screenplay by* Howard Dietz and Arthur Kober; *photographed by* James Wong Howe; *edited by* George Bocmier; *music by* Rodgers and Hart, Donaldson and Kahn, and Brown and Freed; *released by* Metro-Goldwyn-Mayer Pictures. Filmed March 1933–March 1934. Running time: 68 minutes. (Laurel and Hardy appear in a brief scene near the end of the film, in which they engage in an "egg fight" with Lupe Velez. Another MGM star-studded extravaganza, the film also features Jimmy Durante and Ted Healy and his Stooges — Moe Howard, Curly Howard, and Larry Fine.)

On the Wrong Trek (April 18, 1936), sound. *Directed by* Charles Parrott (Charley Chase) and Harold Law; *produced by* Hal Roach; *released by* Metro-Goldwyn-Mayer Pictures. Filmed April 1936. Running time: 20 minutes. (In this short, Laurel and Hardy are briefly seen as hitchhikers, attempting to thumb a ride from Charley Chase.)

Pick a Star (May 21, 1937), sound. *Directed by* Edward Sedgwick; *produced by* Hal Roach; *screenplay by* Richard Flournoy, Arthur Vernon Jones, and Thomas J. Dugan; *photographed by* Norbert Brodine and Art Lloyd; *photographic effects by* Roy Seawright; *edited by* William Terhune; *sound by* William Randall; *music by* Arthur Morton and Marvin Hatley; *songs by* Johnny Lange and Fred Stryker, R. Alexander Anderson, and Marvin Hatley; *released by* Metro-Goldwyn-Mayer Pictures. Filmed November 16, 1936–early January 1937. Running time: 70 minutes. (Laurel and Hardy inhabit two brief sequences in this film, which also stars Patsy Kelly, Jack Haley, Mischa Auer, and James Finlayson.)

XI.
Filmography:
The Post-Roach Period
(1939–1951)

The Flying Deuces (October 20, 1939). Code: LT/B3/BS/SS/SE (sound); rating: 6. *Directed by* Edward Sutherland; *produced by* Boris Morros; *supervised by* Joe Nadel; *story and screenplay by* Ralph Spence, Alfred Schiller, Charles Rogers, and Harry Langdon; *photographed by* Art Lloyd; *aerial photography by* Elmer Dyer; *photographic effects by* Howard Anderson; *edited by* Jack Dennis; *art direction by* Boris Leven; *sound by* William Wilmarth; *music by* John Leipold and Leo Shuken; *musical direction by* Edward Paul; *released by* RKO-Radio Pictures. Filmed July 22–early August 1939. Running time: 69 minutes. *Cast:* Stan Laurel, Oliver Hardy, Jean Parker, Reginald Gardner, James Finlayson, Charles Middleton, Clem Wilenchick/Crane Whitley, Jean del Val, Rychard Cramer, Michael Visaroff, Monica Bannister, Bonnie Bannon, Mary Jane Carey, Christine Babanne, Frank Clarke, Eddie Borden, Sam Lufkin, Kit Guard, Billy Engle, Jack Chefe.

The Flying Deuces was made during a period in which Laurel and Hardy were negotiating a new contract with Hal Roach (resulting in the production of *A Chump at Oxford* and *Saps at Sea*). Material from this film is included in the text, since *The Flying Deuces* was technically produced during the Roach period and features many of the actors from the Roach stock company. Visually, the film resembles the earlier product, as Art Lloyd, who served as cinematographer for dozens of the Roach films, also photographed this film. *The Flying Deuces* is the only non–Roach production that can be referred to as a quality Laurel and Hardy motion picture.

After the team appeared in *Saps at Sea* for Roach, they made the grave mistake of forming their own company, Laurel and Hardy Feature Productions, refusing to sign another contract with their former employer (since Roach insisted upon having each actor on a separate contract). Stan Laurel was looking forward to enjoying complete artistic freedom as a filmmaker, and had developed ideas for several feature films. However, in the commercial atmosphere of Hollywood, Laurel and Hardy found studios with strict policies regarding film content and a very narrow conception of what comedy should be.

In the early 1940s, screen comedy was undergoing a metamorphosis — Buster Keaton, Harold Lloyd, and Harry Langdon had all been out of style for ten years, and Chaplin was making films that were radically different from those he had released during his prime. The Marx Brothers also found it difficult to make a good comedy, completing their last notable film, *The Big Store,* in 1941. W.C. Fields also appeared in his last film of any real interest, *Never Give a Sucker an Even Break,* in 1941, and, within a few years, was dead.

This period in American cinema witnessed a different type of popular comedy, embodied in the form of the screwball comedy and the social satire of filmmakers such as Ernst Lubitsch and Preston Sturges. Slapstick was still used, but in a pastiche form. In the 1940s, comedy became "respectable."

On the other hand, the comedy team still existed, but in a slightly different form. This new impulse, embodied in the Universal films of Abbott and Costello and the ever-continuing Columbia shorts of the Three Stooges, encouraged verbosity and utter *loudness* over the more pantomimic visual technique of performers like Chaplin, Keaton, and Laurel and Hardy. After Abbott and Costello became popular (enough to save Universal from bankruptcy in the early 1940s), subtlety was forever gone from the comedy film — Bud Abbott, the wise-cracking, fast-talking straight man, replaced the slow-burn, methodical Oliver Hardy, and the forever screaming, raucous Lou Costello filled the space that the mime of Stan Laurel used to inhabit. Although Abbott and Costello combined the visual with the

Opposite: **Laurel and Hardy take a break during the shooting of their first non–Roach feature,** *The Flying Deuces* **(1939).**

verbal, and did perform some amazing routines of verbal patter, their comedy has dated, simply because of its dependence on deliberate *jokes,* rather than the comic depiction of everyday human events. Most of this team's films consist of threadbare plots combined with burlesque material and lengthy musical numbers—filler that usually hampers the movement of the narrative. *Abbott and Costello Meet Frankenstein* (1948), which smoothly integrates straight horror scenes with brilliantly performed verbal *and* visual comedy, is a notable exception.

In fact, Abbott and Costello borrowed many gags from the Laurel and Hardy films of the 1940s, not to mention a selection of classic routines from the Roach period. Several gags in *The Dancing Masters* (1943) and *The Bullfighters* (1945) are reworked by Abbott and Costello in their films *Abbott and Costello in Hollywood* (1945) and *Mexican Hayride* (1948). Not only did this team appear to appropriate Laurel and Hardy material for its own productions, it chose second-rate gags that were uninspired when performed by Stan and Ollie.

In the late 1940s, films in the Abbott and Costello style of comedy would be carried to further extremes by Dean Martin and Jerry Lewis, annihilating any trace of subtlety in execution that had been preserved from the classic era. Instead of portraying individuals who are backward because of insufficient psychological development, the Abbott and Costello/Martin and Lewis approach to acting emphasizes sheer idiocy, and, in the pathos of Lou Costello and Jerry Lewis, a purely maudlin version of the infantile Stan Laurel cry.

It was in this milieu of changing tastes and generic formulas that Laurel and Hardy attempted to obtain support for an independent filmmaking company. When Laurel reached an agreement with Twentieth Century–Fox in 1941, he believed that he would be given the freedom of expression that he had always sought. Instead, while they were working on the six films for the studio (and, subsequently, two for MGM), Laurel was not allowed to obtain any authorial position.

The decision for film content was left to a group of studio writers who, because of an unfamiliarity with the team's methods, resorted to simply rehashing routines from their prime films. After experiencing a great degree of freedom and working as active filmmakers for over a decade, the Hollywood Studio System reduced Laurel and Hardy to the status of studio contract players.

Basically, Laurel and Hardy made the same film six different times at Twentieth Century–Fox. All of these productions feature screenplays which are essentially variations on a single generic formula: a group of gangsters engaging in illegal activities becomes involved with a young couple (the perpetual Hollywood love interest) and the Boys. A mob uses Stan and Ollie as pawns in five of the films, with the military filling this role in *Great Guns* (1941). As Stan and Ollie muddle through the criminal activities, they befriend and aid a couple who are falling in love, and wish to get married, in most of the films. The two films made for Metro-Goldwyn-Mayer during this period, *Air-Raid Wardens* (1943) and *Nothing But Trouble* (1945), contain similar variations on these plot devices. While at Roach Studios, the team made films about their characters, with the action emanating from the consequences of their relationship. In all eight of these films, the relationship of Stan and Ollie is controlled by insipid plot contrivances, relegating the Boys to a secondary position, so that they may provide comedy filler for a separate narrative structure.

In one sense, these productions are not Laurel and Hardy films at all, but merely examples of the kind of films Hollywood studios were making in order to aid the United States war effort. In an industry that even depicted Tarzan, Sherlock Holmes, and the Invisible Man battling the Nazis, it is not surprising that they would also enlist the characters of Stan and Ollie to do their part. In the Hal Roach films, Laurel and Hardy provide very subtle social commentary, unintentionally, *naturally,* through the behavior of their characters. In these films, an industry overtaken by patriotism proceeds to bludgeon viewers, expecting to see comedy, with wartime ideology. Taking all these aspects into consideration, the six Fox and two MGM productions possibly constitute the worst series of comedy films to be made by a major Hollywood studio during the classic era.

Great Guns (October 10, 1941). Rating: 3. *Directed by* Monty Banks; *produced by* Sol M. Wurtzel; *screenplay by* Lou Breslow; *photographed by* Glen MacWilliams; *edited by* Al de Gaetano; *art direction by* Richard Day and Albert Hosgett; *set decorations by* Thomas

Little; *costumes by* Herschel; *sound by* W.D. Flick and Harry M. Leonard; *music by* Emil Newman; *released by* Twentieth Century–Fox Pictures. Filmed July 11–early August 1941. Running time: 74 minutes. *Cast:* Stan Laurel, Oliver Hardy, Mae Marsh, Ethel Griffies, Sheila Ryan, Dick Nelson, Edmund MacDonald, Charles Trowbridge, Kane Richmond, Paul Harvey, Charles Arndt, Ludwig Stossel, Pierre Watkin, Dick Rich, Russell Hicks, Billy Benedict; Dave Willock, Irving Bacon, Chet Brandenberg, Alan Ladd.

Inspired by the success of Abbott and Costello's *Buck Privates* earlier that same year, Twentieth Century–Fox decided to place Laurel and Hardy into a film of a similar nature, resulting in *Great Guns.* The studio spent as much on a huge advertising campaign, announcing "The Return of Laurel and Hardy," as they did on the film's insufficient budget.

Stan and Ollie serve as chauffeur and gardener to a young millionaire who is drafted into the United States Army. In order to look after him, the Boys enlist, are sent to basic training in Texas (where they are harassed by the stereotypical sergeant), and aid the Army in carrying out training maneuvers.

A great deal of this film is a poor imitation of the team's classic *Pack Up Your Troubles* and other military parodies of the period. Laurel and Hardy are not afforded many opportunities to exhibit their characterizations, but they do manage to salvage a few good moments out of a very poorly written screenplay. One sequence, involving Stan and Ollie masquerading as a pair of wealthy eccentrics, allows them to develop their characters to a certain extent, but is still far too brief to be satisfying. Much like the films that would follow at Fox, *Great Guns* dedicates a great deal of time to the love affair between the unlikely Army recruit (portrayed by Dick Nelson, whose performance is arguably one of the worst on film) and a woman who works at the military base (Sheila Ryan).

A potentially funny gag in the film is a recreation of a classic routine used by Laurel and Hardy in *The Finishing Touch,* in which Stan carries a long wooden plank from the left of the frame to the

Opposite: **Laurel and Hardy look more like Abbott and Costello in their first Twentieth Century–Fox release, *Great Guns* (1941). Inspired by the latter team's *Buck Privates,* the film features the military themes that would become so prevalent in Hollywood films during the World War II years.**

right, appearing on both sides of the board. This surreal image was first seen in one of Laurel's solo films, *The Noon Whistle,* in 1923. In *Great Guns,* however, it is used three times, forming a triple gag that would have worked much better as a single comic incident (as it did in the earlier films).

A-Haunting We Will Go (August 7, 1942). Rating: 0. *Directed by* Alfred Werker; *produced by* Sol M. Wurtzel; *story by* Lou Breslow and Stanley Rauh; *screenplay by* Lou Breslow; *photographed by* Glen Mac-Williams; *edited by* Alfred Day; *art direction by* Richard Day and Lewis Creber; *set decorations by* Thomas Little; *sound by* Arthur von Kirbach and Harry M. Leonard; *music by* Emil Newman; *released by* Twentieth Century–Fox Pictures. Filmed March 15–early April 1942. Running time: 67 minutes. *Cast:* Stan Laurel, Oliver Hardy, Harry A. Jansen, Sheila Ryan, John Shelton, Don Costello, Elisha Cook, Jr., Edward Gargan, Addison Richards, George Lynn, James Bush, Lou Lubin, Robert Emmett Keane, Richard Lane, Mantan Moreland, Willie Best.

A-Haunting We Will Go is so bad that it makes one wonder how Laurel and Hardy suffered through what must have been a completely frustrating experience. Every second of this film contains conventional material which can be seen in any poverty row feature of the period and none of it is funny in the least.

Stan and Ollie are vagrants who are hired by gangsters to transport a coffin containing a body (actually a criminal on the lam) by train to Dayton, Ohio. En route, the Boys are swindled by two men selling the "Inflato" (a novelty store device which transforms a single dollar into a hundred) and meet Danté the Magician, who hires them to appear with him in his Dayton show. During Danté's "show of illusions," the gangsters are apprehended by the police and the token romantic interest (Sheila Ryan and John Shelton) is firmly established.

Forty of the film's 67 minutes are dedicated to material that does not directly pertain to the actions of Stan and Ollie, instead focusing on the criminal gang and the performances of Danté the Magician. Scenes which do feature the team are poorly executed, consisting of revised gags from *One Good Turn, Scram,* and *On the Wrong Trek*

Opposite: Ollie and Stan appear as stooges in the magic act of Danté the Magician in what is, debatably, the worst Laurel and Hardy film, *A-Haunting We Will Go* (1942).

and, at one point, a ludicrous patriotic speech by Ollie, who claims that, by using Inflato, he can cure the economic and social problems of the world.

Air Raid Wardens (April 1943). Rating: 3. *Directed by* Edward Sedgwick; *produced by* B.F. Zeidman; *screenplay by* Martin Rackin, Jack Jevne, Charles Rogers, and Harry Crane; *photographed by* Walter Lundin; *edited by* Irvine Warburton; *art direction by* Cedric Gibbons; *set decorations by* Edwin B. Willis and Alfred Spencer; *sound by* Douglas Shearer; *music by* Nathaniel Shilkret; *released by* Metro-Goldwyn-Mayer Pictures. Filmed December 1, 1942–early January 1943. Running time: 67 minutes. *Cast:* Stan Laurel, Oliver Hardy, Edgar Kennedy, Jacqueline White, Stephen McNally, Russell Hicks, Nella Walker, Howard Freeman, Donald Meek, Henry O'Neill, Paul Stanton, Robert Emmett O'Connor, Lee Phelps, Martin Cichy, Bert Moorhouse, Don Costello, William Tannen, Forrest Taylor, Edward Hearn, Milton Kibbee, Philip Van Zandt, Frederic Worlock, Betty Jaynes, Howard Mitchell, Jack Gardner, Charles Coleman, Jules Cowles, Rose Hobart, Nolan Leary, Walter Coughlin, Robert Burns, Joe Yule, Sr., Constance Purdy, Daisy (dog).

Their second film to deal with military preparedness, *Air Raid Wardens* is an improvement on *Great Guns* in that MGM provided slightly better production values than were available to them at Fox Studios. Also, writers Jack Jevne and Charles Rogers, cinematographer Walter Lundin, and composer Nathaniel Shilkret, who all worked on several of the Roach period films, helped to make this film slightly better than the others.

Air Raid Wardens begins with the Boys, unable to run a successful business, attempting to enlist in the armed forces. After all branches of the service refuse their enlistment (which is not difficult to imagine, especially in Ollie's case), they land jobs as air raid wardens. One evening when the Boys are ordered to make sure that all lights are out during a test raid, they come up against Joe Bledsoe (Edgar Kennedy), who refuses to darken his home. A slapstick confrontation occurs in which Stan, Ollie, and Bledsoe toss household items at one another. After being discharged because of apparent intoxication, the Boys save a magnesium plant from being sabotaged by a gang of Nazi agents.

The most blatantly propagandistic of their 1940s efforts, *Air*

Raid Wardens contains some genuinely humorous ideas, but most are executed in an uninspired manner. The presence of Edgar Kennedy, who appears in many early films with Laurel and Hardy, adds a trace of respectability to the cast, but he appears tired and his scenes with the Boys are disappointing.

Jitterbugs (June 11, 1943). Rating: 4. *Directed by* Malcolm St. Clair; *produced by* Sol M. Wurtzel; *screenplay by* W. Scott Darling; *photographed by* Lucien Androit; *photographic effects by* Fred Sersen; *edited by* Norman Colbert; *art direction by* James Basevi and Chester Gore; *costumes by* N'Was McKenzie; *sound by* E. Clayton Ward and Harry M. Leonard; *music by* Emil Newman; *songs by* Charles Newman and Lew Pollack; *released by* Twentieth Century–Fox Pictures. Filmed February 15–late March 1943. Running time: 74 minutes. *Cast:* Stan Laurel, Oliver Hardy, Vivian Blaine, Robert Bailey, Lee Patrick, Francis Ford, Douglas Fowley, Robert Emmett Keane, Noel Madison, Charles Halton.

Jitterbugs is probably the best of Laurel and Hardy's 1940s output, featuring a glimmer of the classic Stan and Ollie relationship. The first third resembles their earlier films to some extent, with the Boys, a two-man zoot-suit band, attempting to pilot a dilapidated old auto and travel trailer through blistering desert heat.

When Stan and Ollie run out of gasoline, a young entrepreneur, Chester Wright (Robert Bailey), stops to aid them, introducing his answer to the problem of rationing—a pill which transforms water into gasoline. Giving them a can of actual gas, Wright convinces them that he has performed a miracle. Joining them, the young con artist proposes to use their show as a front to sell his false product, but soon meets and falls in love with Susan Cowan (Vivian Blaine), a beautiful young woman whose mother has been cheated out of ten thousand dollars by a gang of criminals. Stan and Ollie join Wright in his plot to steal the money back from the gangsters and, after several semi-dangerous escapades, they emerge triumphant. Ignoring the Boys, Wright exits with his newly won sweetheart, leaving the two rejected clowns floating in the ocean.

Jitterbugs is the only film in this series that allows Laurel and Hardy some scope to develop their performances. Posing as a Southern colonel and his English valet, they get to do some real acting, with Laurel using his "Lord Paddington" voice from *A Chump*

at Oxford. Laurel also revises his characterization from *Another Fine Mess,* impersonating a wealthy society woman who retrieves the stolen money for Ms. Cowan.

Although there are some interesting moments, the film still resembles the other productions in every respect, with 15 minutes being dedicated to the singing of Vivian Blaine. In sequences which do not even remotely include Laurel and Hardy, musical performances are poorly staged (one of which is an unrelated propaganda number, featuring a group of leggy women promoting war bonds). Most of the material in *Jitterbugs* is also featured in the earlier films of this series, with the gas pill being a carbon copy of the "Inflato" gimmick in *A-Haunting We Will Go.* There are also reworked gags from *That's My Wife, Perfect Day, Our Relations,* and *Block-Heads* in this film.

The Dancing Masters (November 19, 1943). Rating: 3. *Directed by* Malcolm St. Clair; *produced by* Lee Marcus; *story by* George Bricker; *screenplay by* W. Scott Darling; *photographed by* Norbert Brodine; *photographic effects by* Fred Sersen; *edited by* Norman Colbert; *art direction by* James Basevi and Chester Gore; *set decorations by* Thomas Little and Al Orenbach; *sound by* Bernard Freericks and Harry M. Leonard; *music by* Arthur Lange; *musical direction by* Emil Newman; *released by* Twentieth Century–Fox Pictures. Filmed June 1–25, 1943. Running time: 63 minutes. *Cast:* Stan Laurel, Oliver Hardy, Trudy Marshall, Robert Bailey, Matt Briggs, Margaret Dumont, Allan Lane, Daphne Pollard, Charley Rogers, Hank Mann, Emory Parnell, Robert Emmett Keane, Robert Mitchum.

The Dancing Masters is a hybrid of the classic Stan and Ollie characterizations and conventional Hollywood gag structures. In this film, the performances of Laurel and Hardy seem much more natural than in some of the earlier Twentieth Century–Fox pictues, and Stan is allowed to frequently indulge in his famous rhetoric-strangle routines ("The harder they fall, the bigger I am"). However, *The Dancing Masters,* like the other films in this series, concentrates more on plot than on situation or character, stifling the atmosphere that the team attempts to create through characterization. The bulk

Opposite: Drag queen Stan adjusts Ollie's tie in the best of the Twentieth Century–Fox films, *Jitterbugs* (1943).

of the film deals with the romantic interest (Trudy Marshall and Robert Bailey) and a totally superfluous gang of thugs. The plot concerns a young inventor's attempt to obtain corporate financing for "the Invisible Ray," a weapon of mass destruction which can be used against enemies of the United States. Dance instructors Stan and Ollie befriend the inventor and attempt to aid him in his machinations. A typical Hollywood propaganda statement, this aspect of the film is an outright embarrassment to the integrity of Laurel and Hardy, depicting the Boys as supporting war armaments dealers. *The Dancing Masters* constituted the third "war effort" film they had appeared in since leaving Roach Studios.

The film does include some interesting moments, however, but most of these are reworked gags from some of the best Roach films, including *The Battle of the Century, Perfect Day, Hog Wild, County Hospital, Thicker Than Water,* and *Block-Heads.*

The Big Noise (October 1944). Rating: 1. *Directed by* Malcolm St. Clair; *produced by* Sol M. Wurtzel; *screenplay by* W. Scott Darling; *photographed by* Joe MacDonald; *photographic effects by* Fred Sersen; *edited by* Norman Colbert; *art direction by* Lyle Wheeler and John Ewing; *set decorations by* Thomas Little and Al Orenbach; *costumes by* Yvonne Wood; *makeup by* Guy Pierce; *sound by* Bernard Freericks and Harry M. Leonard; *music by* David Buttolph and Cyril J. Mockridge; *musical direction by* Emil Newman; *released by* Twentieth Century–Fox Pictures. Filmed April 1944. Running time: 74 minutes. *Cast:* Stan Laurel, Oliver Hardy, Robert Blake, Jack Norton, Veda Ann Borg, Doris Merrick, Arthur Space, Esther Howard, Robert Duddley, Francis Ford, Charles C. Wilson, George Melford, Frank Fenton, James Bush, Philip Van Zandt, Del Henderson, Louis Arco, Beal Wong, Edgar Dearing, Selmer Jackson, Harry Hayden, Julie Carter, Sarah Edwards, Emmett Vogan, Ken Christy, Billy Bletcher.

Almost as bad as *A-Haunting We Will Go* and identical in many ways to *The Dancing Masters, The Big Noise* has Stan and Ollie once again wading through propaganda in an effort to protect war armaments. Stan Laurel actually attempted to suggest some gag ideas to W. Scott Darling, author of the screenplay, but was totally ignored.

Stan and Ollie, mail-order detectives who wear dearstalker caps and smoke meerschaum pipes, are hired by an eccentric inventor

(Arthur Space) to transport a powerful new bomb to Washington, D.C. During the trip to the nation's capital, they are pursued by gangsters (who want to sell the weapon to the Axis, of course) and stumble into a remote-controlled airplane that the Army is using to practice defensive maneuvers. The Boys emerge triumphant, however, by exploding a Japanese submarine with the bomb.

Another embarrassing project for Laurel and Hardy, *The Big Noise* offers absolutely nothing new for the team to perform. The gangster plot is again stressed, with the romantic interest provided by a a seven-time widow who briefly falls in love with Ollie (one of several subplots that are developed but never concluded). Laurel and Hardy both appear to be extremely lethargic in this film, as does the rest of the cast. W. Scott Darling's screenplay is pretentious and stilted, with characters stopping in the midst of comic scenes to recite a few lines of blatant jingoism. The final sequence is amateurish and insulting, with Stan and Ollie destroying the "Jap" submarine. It is difficult to imagine even patriotic wartime audiences enjoying this static and unfunny film, which includes reconstructions of gags from *Berth Marks, Oliver the Eighth,* and *The Flying Deuces.*

Nothing But Trouble (March 1945). Rating: 2. *Directed by* Sam Taylor; *produced by* B.F. Zeidman; *screenplay by* Russell Rouse and Ray Golden; *additional dialogue by* Bradford Ropes and Margaret Gruen; *photographed by* Charles Salerno, Jr.; *edited by* Conrad A. Nervig; *art direction by* Cedric Gibbons and Harry McAfee; *set decorations by* Edwin B. Willis and Jack Bonar; *costumes by* Irene; *sound by* Douglas Shearer and Thomas Edwards; *music by* Nathaniel Shilkret; *released by* Metro-Goldwyn-Mayer Pictures. Filmed October 1944. Running time: 70 minutes. *Cast:* Stan Laurel, Oliver Hardy, Henry O'Neill, Mary Boland, David Leland, John Warburton, Matthew Boulton, Connie Gilchrist, Philip Merivale, Paul Porcasi, Jean de Briac, Joe Yule, Sr., Eddie Dunn, Forbes Murray, Ray Teal, Howard Mitchell, Steve Darrell, William Frambe, Garry Owen, Robert Emmett O'Connor, Robert Emmett Homans, William J. Holmes, Mayo Newhall, Toby Noolan, Chester Clute.

Laurel and Hardy's second film for Metro-Goldwyn-Mayer, *Nothing But Trouble* features Laurel and Hardy reprising their servant roles from their 1928 short, *From Soup to Nuts.* The film is pleasing to look at, with adequate art direction by Cedric Gibbons, but also relies heavily upon tried-and-true gag material.

The Boys are chef and butler to a wealthy couple (Henry O'Neill and Mary Boland) who are housing an exiled boy king (David Leland) from the mythical country of Orlandia. After attempting to escape the clutches of his evil guardian (Philip Merivale), the boy has several harrowing experiences, but is saved in the end by Stan and Ollie.

Originally entitled *The Home Front,* this film includes the patriotic zeal of the earlier 1940s efforts, this time in the form of the boy king who sentimenally preaches about American democracy. Laurel and Hardy once again play subordinate roles, with the main narrative concern being the story of the king and his guardian, Prince Saul (who supplies the criminal element). The Boys spend a lot of screen time simply running about from one place to another, stealing a piece of meat from a lion's cage at the zoo (which they prepare for a society dinner), and languishing in jail. The final scene, in which Stan and Ollie teeter on a window ledge, recalls a gag used in one of their finest films, *Liberty,* made 16 years earlier.

The Bullfighters (May 18, 1945). Rating: 1. *Directed by* Malcolm St. Clair; *produced by* William Girard; *screenplay by* W. Scott Darling; *photographed by* Norbert Brodine; *photographic effects by* Fred Sersen; *edited by* Stanley Rabjohn; *art direction by* Lyle Wheeler and Chester Gore; *set decorations by* Thomas Little and Al Orenbach; *costumes by* Bonnie Cashin; *makeup by* Ben Nye; sound by Arthur von Kirbach and Harry M. Leonard; *music by* David Buttolph; *musical direction by* Emil Newman; *released by* Twentieth Century-Fox Pictures. Filmed Mid-November–December 16, 1944. Running time: 69 minutes. *Cast:* Stan Laurel, Oliver Hardy, Margo Woode, Richard Lane, Carol Andrews, Diosa Costello, Frank McCown/Rory Calhoun, Ralph Sanford, Irving Gump, Edward Gargan, Lorraine de Wood, Emmett Vogan, Roger Neury, Guy Zanette, Robert W. Filmer, Francisco Reyas, Daniel Rea, Max Wagner, Julian Rivero, Jose Portugal, Gus Glassmire, Hank Worden, Steve Darrell, Jose Dominguez, Ralph Platz, Raphael Storm, Jay Novello, Cyril Ring, Paul Kruger, Henry Russell, Edgar Mason.

A complete artistic insult, it is fortunate that *The Bullfighters* was Laurel and Hardy's final American film. The team's inability to control their own film content is very apparent, with their performances reaching an unparalleled level of self-parody. The characters of Stan and Ollie in this film look like they are being portrayed by Laurel and Hardy impersonators — the two men are completely uninspired, merely walking through material they had performed with consummate expertise years earlier.

Stan and Ollie are detectives from Peoria, Illinois, who are sent to Mexico City in search of Larceny Nell, a wanted criminal. When they arrive, the Boys find out that Richard K. Muldoon (Ralph Sanford), an innocent man they had sent to prison eight years earlier, is in town, vowing to "skin them alive" if he ever meets them again. Blackmailed by one of Muldoon's henchmen, Stan agrees to impersonate Don Sebastian, a famous bullfighter who looks exactly like the "guy from Peoria." When the real Sebastian arrives on the scene, Laurel portrays both characters, but is given little opportunity to do any real acting.

The bullfight sequence (which involves both Sebastian and Stan) consists of long shots from the Rouben Mamoulian film, *Blood and Sand* (1940), juxtaposed with poorly composed medium shots of Laurel swinging a matador's cape. The scene has no continuity whatsoever, with the figure in the long shots appearing a head taller than Stan. After Muldoon recognizes Stan, the detective, he follows the Boys back to their hotel, where he eventually confronts them in their room. The final scene is an extremely tasteless variation on the team's earlier physical distortion gags, with Stan and Ollie's talking heads sitting atop skeleton bodies. "Here's another nice mess you've gotten me into," says Ollie, as Stan cries.

Containing several minutes of filler in the form of musical numbers, *The Bullfighters* also includes reworkings of situations from *You're Darn Tootin', Angora Love, Blotto, Pack Up Your Troubles, Hollywood Party, Going Bye-Bye, The Live Ghost, The Fixer-Uppers,* and *Our Relations*.

Atoll K (November 21, 1951 — French release). (Released in the United States as *Robinson Crusoeland* and reissued in 1954 as *Utopia*.) Rating: 5. *Directed by* Leo Joannon and John Berry; *assistant direction by* Isabelle Kloukowski, Jean-Claude Eger, and Alfred Goulding; *produced by* Raymond Eger; *supervised by* Paul Joly; *based on a story by* Leo Joannon; *screenplay by* Rene Wheeler and P. Tellini; *photographed by* Armand Thiraro and Louis Nee; *edited by* Raymond Isnardon;

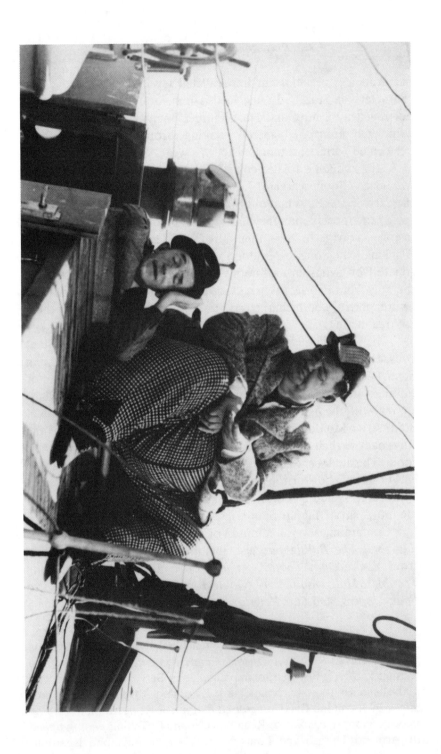

music by Paul Misraki. A co-production of Les Films Sirius, Paris, Franco-London Films S.A., Paris, and Fortezza Film, Rome. Filmed August 1950–March 1951. Running time: 98 minutes (European release); 82 minutes (American release). *Cast:* Stan Laurel, Oliver Hardy, Suzy Delair, Max Elloy, Suzet Mais, Felix Oudart, Robert Murzeau, Luigi Tosi, Michael Dalmatoff, Adriano Rimoldi, Charles Lemontier, Simone Viosin, Olivia Hussenot, Lucien Callamand, Robert Vattier, Gilbert Morfau, Jean Verner, Andre Randall, C. May, R. Legris, Paul Frees (narrator, American release).

A conglomeration of slapstick comedy, drama, and political commentary, *Atoll K* is a very confusing, but strangely compelling, film. Shot near Cannes, France, and co-produced by independent French and Italian firms, this production could not have been made in the United States of the early 1950s. Co-director John Berry was under investigation by the communist-hunting House Committee on Un-American Activities when the socialist-tinged screenplay was written in 1949.

The film opens with Stan and Ollie in London, where they inherit a large sum of money (most of which is taken for taxes by three European governments), an old yacht, and a South Pacific island. After taking aboard a stateless man, who is not claimed by any country, and a stowaway, the Boys sail for their newly inherited home. En route, a raging storm scuttles their boat against the shore of a volcanic atoll, where they decide to establish permanent residency. Stan, Ollie, and their two new friends work the land, plant crops, and build a couple of shacks in which to cook and sleep. Soon, Cherie, a young French woman who has fled from her fiancé, arrives on the island, becoming the first female inhabitant. To insure that progress continues unabated, the four men agree to treat Cherie as an equal, not as a romantic object.

Soon, an expedition lands, discovering large deposits of uranium. The leader of the group (Cherie's fiancé) reports to the inhabitants that some government will soon claim sovereignty of the atoll in an effort to extract the uranium (presumably to use in the construction of nuclear weapons). The Boys realize that Antoine,

Opposite: Stan and Ollie aboard ship in the team's last screen effort, the French-Italian co-production *Atoll K* (1951).

their "stateless" friend, was the first of their group to set foot on the island, therefore exempting any country from claiming possession of Atoll K.

Ollie provides a further safeguard against colonial takeover by drafting a constitution, forbidding the use of laws, taxes, money, prisons, and the issuing of passports. Christening the atoll Crusoeland and raising a flag, the Boys declare it to be a truly free country. Ollie is elected as President, the two men and the woman are appointed as his cabinet, and Stan is designated as "The People."

Word of this utopia spreads fast, and Crusoeland is soon invaded by immigrants seeking a better life under Ollie's system of political and social equality. Paradise lasts only a short time, however, with Ollie being forced to create a body of laws to suppress the violent actions of a number of new immigrants. This act creates a state of vigilantism among the people, who capture President Ollie and his cabinet, ordering that all be hanged the following morning. As the execution is about to be carried out, a violent storm floods the atoll, completely submerging it. The Boys and their companions are saved, however, by the gallows platform which floats like a raft.

The final scene of the film shows Cherie being reunited with her fiancé and the two men back in the world of oppression (Antoine is presumably eaten as he tries to board a ship while hiding in a lion cage). The last shot features Stan and Ollie, now living on their South Sea island, being harassed by government officials who drop by to impound all of their belongings.

Atoll K is the only Laurel and Hardy film (other than the 1940s productions made during World War II) that features outspoken political pretensions. A mixture of anti-imperialist and anti-nuclear sentiments, it presents a very pessimistic attitude toward postwar society, an aspect that sometimes fails to gel with the comedy material of Laurel and Hardy. The two political idealists with whom the Boys establish their utopia are either silenced or dead at the end of this film, with Stan and Ollie exiled to a small island where they are refused even the barest of necessities.

This commentary is interesting, but it is not part of a *natural* outgrowth of the Stan and Ollie relationship, as are the sociocultural elements in their Roach films. These attitudes are part of the muddled screenplay, and do not appear to fit the mentalities of the Stan and Ollie characters. For example, one scene includes Stan stating a conglomeration of confused rhetoric, ending with a statement about the undesirability of paying taxes. It can be said that the film's denouement does provide a logical conclusion to the relationship established between the two characters in the Roach films—they are completely alone together, not only in the world of their infantile mentalities, but in their own physical world as well.

Unlike their 1940s American films, which champion a narrow-minded political ideology, *Atoll K* presents what appears to be a much more objective world view. Several different socioeconomic and political structures are depicted in the film, including capitalism, collectivism, and anarchy, but none are successful. *Atoll K* possesses the most politically correct viewpoint possible—no existing system of government can be completely effective because of the subjective experience of individual human beings.

The most distressing aspect of *Atoll K* is the physical appearance of Laurel and Hardy. During production of the film, Laurel's diabetes flared up and he also underwent an operation in a Paris hospital in order to have a prostate growth removed. Only 60 years old at the time, the actor looks much worse in the film than he did at his death in 1965 at the age of 74. Hardy also experienced heat exhaustion and an irregular heartbeat due to an escalating weight problem. Originally scheduled to be shot in 12 weeks, the production of *Atoll K* took eight months to complete because of the team's health problems and miscommunication between members of the multilingual cast and crew. It is unfortunate that the film was not produced a few years later, when both Laurel and Hardy were in much better health and more care could have been lavished upon the script and performances. Stan Laurel referred to the film as "an abortion," claiming that "no one knew what in the hell was going on."[1]

The inability of an international cast to communicate properly is evident in the finished film, with a dubbed soundtrack that is hopelessly inadequate. The Boys do provide some good comedy, however, with Stan engaging in his beloved rhetoric strangle, playing with his pet lobster, and shaving himself with a sheet of sandpaper, and Ollie making a perceptive comment about their long-term relationship. When Stan complains about shipboard conditions, Ollie gently asks, "Haven't I always taken care of you? You're the first one I think of."

As Laurel stated, *Atoll K* is an abortion in some respects, but it is much better than any of their 1940s films—the production does not rely upon reworked gags and is a narrative change of pace for the team. Their characters, although looking old and somewhat sickly, do act like the Stan and Ollie of their earlier work, providing a pleasant atmosphere throughout much of the film. Sometimes a painful viewing experience, *Atoll K* must be judged as a failed, but interesting, experiment.

Laurel and Hardy gave cameo performances in one short film during the post–Roach period:

The Tree in a Test Tube (1943). *Directed by* Charles MacDonald; *produced by* The Forest Service of the United States Department of Agriculture; *photographed in* 16mm color by A.H.C. Sintzenich; *edited by* Boris Vermont; *sound by* Reuben Ford; *music by* Edward Craig; *released by* Twentieth Century–Fox Pictures. Filmed February–March 1943. Running time: 10 minutes. *Cast:* Stan Laurel, Oliver Hardy, Pete Smith and Lee Vickers (narrators).

This documentary film includes a few silent scenes featuring Laurel and Hardy combined with footage of factories, laboratories, and military bases located in the United States. Made by the Department of Agriculture as a boost to the war effort, the film stresses the need for prioritizing the uses of wood taken from American forests. The Boys are shown displaying many everyday objects made from forest materials, and are allowed to clown a little when Ollie suggests that Stan's head is also made out of wood. Along with the "lost" two-strip technicolor *The Rogue Song, The Tree in a Test Tube* constitutes the team's only other color film.

XII.
A Final Word

"I think popular culture in America
has become another kind of junk food;
our television, our music, most of our
films, our politicians, our architecture,
most of it is very mediocre and junky."
—Woody Allen (April 28, 1979)[1]

Looking back at the films in which they had appeared in the
1940s, Stan Laurel once stated, "We had no say in those films, and
it sure looked it. We had done too many films in our own way for
us to keep taking anything like that, so we gave up the ghost. It was
sickening."[2]

In order to escape the stifling atmosphere of Hollywood, Laurel
and Hardy signed an agreement with a booking agent to do a nine-
month tour of British music halls in 1947. Returning to the milieu of
his early days as a performer, Laurel was again able to create comedy
material and perform it in classic style with his partner. After completing *Atoll K* and returning to the United States to allow Laurel to
regain his health, the team once again toured Britain for a nine-
month period in 1952, and again in 1953. These tours provided
Laurel and Hardy with the freedom they had sought after ending
their association with Hal Roach in 1940. It is unfortunate, however,
that these performances were not preserved on film.

One last opportunity to create their own motion pictures was
offered to them by Hal Roach, Jr., in 1955. Laurel agreed to the offer,
with the stipulation that he and Hardy would work under conditions
similar to those during their previous association with Roach Studios.
Four one-hour films were to be made, for release to television, containing material featuring Laurel's white-magic gags. Believing that
a fairytale setting would be perfect for the childlike characters of
Stan and Ollie, Laurel was enthusiastic about beginning work on the

141

films. However, further illness and the death of Oliver Hardy on August 7, 1957, prevented the project from getting under way.

On the occasion of Hardy's passing, Laurel said, "He was like a brother to me. We seemed to sense each other."[3] Although Laurel and Hardy had not become close personal friends until their music hall tours, it seems that, in reality, they were somewhat like the characters they had portrayed in the films. One of the aspects the men shared with their cinematic creations was their problems with marriage—Stan Laurel was married seven times (thrice to the same woman), with Oliver Hardy only taking the vows a total of three times. Also, like the confrontations with authority that Stan and Ollie had on screen, they experienced a large degree of disappointment from having their cinematic aspirations dashed by the production processes of the Hollywood studios. Stan Laurel was rewarded by the industry with a special Academy Award for "creative pioneering in the field of cinema comedy" in 1961. He continued writing comedy material until his death on February 23, 1965.

Although they completed their last "prime" film almost fifty years ago, a revival of interest in the team and classic comedy in general has made their films accessible to a new generation of viewers on cable television and video cassette. Obviously, watching classic films on a small screen at home is not comparable to experiencing the event with a live audience in a theater, but the availability of new technology does provide a means for people who wish to see truly humorous and thought-provoking comedy films.

Unlike the comedy of the past, contemporary comic films are targeted toward a much narrower audience. Exemplified in the *schtick* parodies of Mel Brooks and graduates of the "Saturday Night Live" television show, modern filmmakers fail to take comedy seriously, relying on tasteless jokes and situations which are ludicrous instead of humorous. Instead of creating complex characters such as Stan and Ollie, these technicians often devise very one-dimensional, uninteresting character types that are soon forgotten by audiences.

Many contemporary films still utilize the tenets of earlier visual and verbal forms, but usually demonstrate it through the actions of these idiotic stereotyped characters (such as "nerds" or other assorted youthful morons). This type of humor is frequently created at the expense of minority groups, often including overtones of a sexist or racist nature. One viewing of *Animal House, Beverly Hills Cop, Revenge of the Nerds* (and similar fare), or anything with Cheech and Chong, makes this apparent. Unlike the Laurel and Hardy world, which depicts all characters as being equally backward, modern comedy thrives on attacking certain groups of unfortunates.

In Woody Allen, the modern cinema does have an equivalent to the comics of the classic era. Over the years, Allen has combined classic comic technique and content with a humanist philosophy that is absent from the work of other filmmaker-comedians. Allen's humor, which relies upon methods of both visual and stand-up comedy, is an amalgam of the styles of most classic performers, including the Marx Brothers, Charles Chaplin, and Stan Laurel. His approach is the only contemporary one that consistently emphasizes the relationship as the essential aspect of life and the comic possibilities within the complex web of its structure.

Another interesting facet of Allen's comedy that indirectly comments upon the work of Laurel and Hardy is the writer-director's self-reflective approach to the philosophical content of his films. Often criticized by reviewers and fans who long to see more of the early, funny films that he wrote and directed in the late 1960s and early 1970s, instead of the more self-indulgent and didactic works of more recent years, Allen has even made a film, *Stardust Memories* (1980), that explores these issues. Allen, like Chaplin and others, is a filmmaker who has used comedy as a vehicle for social commentary, but he is also an artist who attempts to examine the role of comedy in society and the extent to which it can be used as a philosophical force. Allen has explored the entire comic spectrum, from directing the slapstick *Take the Money and Run* (1970) to the wonderfully nostalgic *The Purple Rose of Cairo* (1985).

Comedy entertains us, but it can also inform and inspire us in many ways. Most fundamentally, comedy facilitates laughter, and humor with transcendent appeal is able to perform this function over the span of many generations. It is this fundamental goal that Stan Laurel and Oliver Hardy hoped to attain, with an approach to comic filmmaking that remains unique to this day. Not all of the films in which this team appeared are outstanding, but their work as a whole presents a laughter-filled world inhabited by two very complex, very *likeable* clowns. Their prime films, intended to provide humor, also indirectly comment upon the world in which we live—perhaps the perfect combination, maintaining a delicate balance between emotion and logic, between heart and mind.

The treatment of the team in 1940s Hollywood provides an example of the way in which our society has regarded the unique talents of such artists—individual creativity must always suffer at the hands of popular culture and the corporate system that is the motion picture industry. An examination of past criticism also provides a look at how our society evaluates the work of artists such as Laurel and Hardy. Hopefully, this text has provided an alternative approach to the way in which the team's films have been viewed.

In 1960, Buster Keaton commented:

> In our day, there was tremendous competition in our field. Today there is none. Jerry Lewis remains on top ... but Jerry doesn't have Chaplin, Lloyd, (Lloyd) Hamilton, and a half a dozen others on his heels ... with Laurel and Hardy coming on apace to reach truly great heights. If our comedy is acceptable today, if the critics rave and the fan letters come in, I think it can be taken for granted that we have contributed to something more than early movies. The laughter of the world?[4]

Notes

I. Why Take Laurel and Hardy Seriously?

1. Charles Barr, *Laurel and Hardy* (Berkeley: University of California Press, 1967), p. 6.
2. Bosley Crowther, *The New York Times* (1939).
3. John McCabe, *Mr. Laurel and Mr. Hardy* (New York: New American Library, 1961), p. 111.
4. Gerald Mast, *The Comic Mind* (Indianapolis: Bobbs, 1973), p. 62.
5. John McCabe, *Laurel and Hardy* (New York: Bonanza Books, 1975), p. 11.
6. John McCabe, *The Comedy World of Stan Laurel* (Garden City: Doubleday and Company, 1974), pp. xii–xiii.

II. Stan Laurel

1. John McCabe, *The Comedy World of Stan Laurel*, p. 208.
2. John McCabe, *Laurel and Hardy*, p. 10.
3. Fred Lawrence Guiles, *Stan: The Life of Stan Laurel* (New York: Stein and Day, 1980), p. 97.
4. John McCabe, *Mr. Laurel and Mr. Hardy*, p. 95.
5. John McCabe, *Laurel and Hardy*, p. 11.

III. Oliver Hardy

1. Ephraim Katz, *The Film Encyclopedia* (New York: Thomas Y. Crowell Publishers, 1979), p. 533.
2. John McCabe, *Mr. Laurel and Mr. Hardy*, p. 44.

IV. Cinematic and Comic Structure

1. John McCabe, *Mr. Laurel and Mr. Hardy,* p. 112.
2. Charles Barr, pp. 33–38.
3. John McCabe, *Mr. Laurel and Mr. Hardy,* p. 86.
4. Raymond Durgnat, "Hoop-de-Doo for Mr. Laurel and Mr. Hardy," *Films and Filming* (November 1965).
5. Charles Barr, p. 21.
6. Andre Bazin, *What Is Cinema?* (Berkeley: University of California Press, 1967), p. 46.
7. Charles Barr, p. 22.
8. John McCabe, *Mr. Laurel and Mr. Hardy,* p. 103.

V. The Boys as Couple

1. John McCabe, *Laurel and Hardy,* p. 16.
2. John McCabe, *Mr. Laurel and Mr. Hardy,* p. 46.
3. Charles Barr, p. 61.
4. Charles Barr, p. 75.
5. John McCabe, *Mr. Laurel and Mr. Hardy,* p. 136.
6. Joseph McBride, *Hawks on Hawks* (Berkeley: University of California Press, 1982), p. 20.
7. Tino Balio, *The American Film Industry* (Madison: The University of Wisconsin Press, 1985), p. 382.
8. Charles Barr, p. 65.

VI. The Boys and Physical Objects

1. Tino Balio, p. 380.

IX. The Boys and Society

1. Charles Barr, p. 58.
2. Charles Barr, p. 30.
3. Gerald Mast, *The Comic Mind,* p. 192.
4. Gerald Mast, p. 192.

XI. Filmography: The Post-Roach Period

1. John McCabe, *Mr. Laurel and Mr. Hardy,* p. 145.

XII. A Final Word

1. Robert Benayoun, *The Films of Woody Allen* (New York: Crown Publishers, Inc., 1985), p. 162.

2. John McCabe, *Mr. Laurel and Mr. Hardy,* p. 143.

3. William Cahn, *Harold Lloyd's World of Comedy* (New York: Deull, Sloan, and Pearce, 1964), p. 287.

Bibliography

Books About Laurel and Hardy

Barr, Charles. *Laurel and Hardy*. Berkeley: University of California Press, 1967.
Everson, William K. *The Films of Laurel and Hardy*. Secaucus: Citadel Press, 1967.
Guiles, Fred Lawrence. *Stan*. New York: Stein and Day Publishers, 1980.
McCabe, John. *The Comedy World of Stan Laurel*. Garden City: Doubleday and Company, 1974.
McCabe, John. *Laurel and Hardy;* text compiled by Al Kilgore, filmography by Richard W. Bann. New York: Bonanza Books, 1975.
McCabe, John. *Mr. Laurel and Mr. Hardy*. New York: New American Library, 1961.
Skretvedt, Randy. *Laurel and Hardy: The Magic Behind the Movies*. Beverly Hills: Moonstone Press, 1987.

Magazine and Newpaper Articles About Laurel and Hardy

Crowther, Bosley. *New York Times*. Film Reviews, 1939.
Durgnat, Raymond. "Hoop-de-Doo for Mr. Laurel and Mr. Hardy." Films and Filming. (November 1965).
Pratfall. Complete Series. Universal City.

Books Featuring Material Directly or Indirectly Related to Laurel and Hardy

Balio, Tino. *The American Film Industry*. Madison: University of Wisconsin Press, 1985.
Bazin, Andre. *What Is Cinema?* Berkeley: University of California Press, 1967.
Benayoun, Robert. *The Films of Woody Allen*. New York: Crown Publishers, Inc., 1985.

Cahn, William. *Harold Lloyd's World of Comedy*. New York: Duell, Sloan, and Pierce, 1964.

Everson, William K. *The Films of Hal Roach*. New York: Museum of Modern Art, 1971.

Katz, Ephraim. *The Film Encyclopedia*. New York: Thomas Y. Crowell Publishers, 1979.

Maltin, Leonard. *Movie Comedy Teams*. New York: New American Library, 1985.

Index

Entry numbers in **boldface** indicate photographs